RELENTLESS
PURSUIT

RELENTLESS PURSUIT

GOD'S LOVE OF OUTSIDERS
INCLUDING THE OUTSIDER IN ALL OF US

KEN GIRE

BETHANY HOUSE PUBLISHERS
a division of Baker Publishing Group
Minneapolis, Minnesota

© 2012 by Ken Gire

Published by Bethany House Publishers
11400 Hampshire Avenue South
Bloomington, Minnesota 55438
www.bethanyhouse.com

Bethany House Publishers is a division of
Baker Publishing Group, Grand Rapids, Michigan

Printed in the United States of America

Library of Congress Cataloging-in-Publication Data

Gire, Ken.
Relentless pursuit : God's love of outsiders (including the outsider in all of us) / Ken Gire.
    p. cm.
Summary: "Popular author uses stories from the Bible and his own life to teach about God's love for those who feel like outsiders"—Provided by publisher.
    ISBN 978-0-7642-0883-6 (pbk. : alk. paper) 1. God (Christianity)—Love. 2. Conversion—Christianity. I. Title.
    BT140.G57 2012
    231.7—dc23
                                    2012006412

Cover design by Gearbox / David Carlson

Author is represented by WordServe Literary Group

12   13   14   15   16   17   18   7   6   5   4   3   2   1

To Greg Johnson
for finding me

No matter how many times we fail, God will never fail us. He knows our frailty and loves us still, pursuing us relentlessly as a lover his beloved.

—Robert Waldron
The Hound of Heaven at My Heels:
The Lost Diaries of Francis Thompson

CONTENTS

PROLOGUE

Leaving Home

This pursuit of the whole mankind and of the Jewish folk in particular is but a larger manifestation of God's way with each individual soul.

—Francis Peter Le Buffe
The Hound of Heaven: An Interpretation

The Bible from start to finish is the story of God's pursuit of the outsider—the foreigner, the stranger, the outcast. From Adam and Eve outside the garden of Eden . . . to Hagar outside the camp of Abraham . . . to Lazarus outside the gate of the rich man. From corner prostitutes to colonized lepers to common thieves. From the down-and-out to the demon-possessed, the Bible is filled with outsiders pursued—and transformed—by God's relentless love.

The pursuit of the whole of humankind is but a larger manifestation of God's way with the individual soul. But God doesn't stop his pursuit when he brings us safely into the fold.

He continues keeping watch over us to see when a part of us, however small or seemingly inconsequential, wanders from him. That part may be a thought that breaks from the flock in search of pastures that seem greener, however forbidden; of waters that seem more plentiful, however dangerous. It may be a part of us that is prone to wander, perhaps not far or for long but far enough and long enough not to hear the Shepherd's voice when he calls. It may be a part that strays one famished night without realizing it, going from one patch of grass to another to another until, finally lifting its head, it sees it is lost. Or it may be a part that feels angry at, even betrayed by, the flock, and, in a headstrong moment, bolts to be free from it.

Even those of us who consider ourselves insiders feel like outsiders at some time or another. Some feel that way all the time. At work and at social gatherings. In their church. Or in their marriage. Each of us, or at least a part of each of us, feels on the outside, looking in. The estranged adolescent. The self-conscious sibling. The abandoned mate. The returning visitor no one remembers, Sunday after awkward Sunday. The man in the wheelchair to whom people nod and smile but don't talk to or shake hands with. The pregnant teenager. The purple-haired boy with sinister-looking tattoos and tribal-like piercings. Those in chronic pain, out of work, widowed, orphaned; single parents, struggling to keep the electricity on. The down-and-out, the mentally ill, living in the littered alleys off cold and indifferent streets. People who are lonely and depressed. People who are disabled, who are elderly, those living on the tattered margins of society. People holed up in some sagging tenement, surrounded by decay, dying of cancer, dying of AIDS.

This book is about the heart of God and the lengths to which his heart goes to find ours, to bundle it up in his arms and to carry it home. It is written from the perspective of the lost sheep. As such, it's not a book for the ninety-nine who are safe as much as for the one who is not. That lost part is surely not the whole of who you are or the whole of who I am, but it is a real part nonetheless.

That this lost part is pursued *by God* reveals our worth.

That it is *relentlessly* pursued reveals how much.

□ □ □　▥

I have felt an outsider much of my life, though for the life of me I couldn't tell you exactly why.

Red hair was part of it. ("Hey, carrot top!" "I'd rather be dead than red on the head.")

Warts that covered my hands one year, inexplicably, then left the next, just as inexplicably—that was part of it too. ("Ew, warts!" "What have you been doing, playing with toads?")

In my old neighborhood I had an identity; I was one of the kids everyone knew and pretty much liked. Though younger than most of the others, I did have a friend my age, which helped. My sister being older gave me some credibility. Finally getting picked for teams secured my insider status.

Status was clear in the old neighborhood. Older kids ruled, but they were pretty good kids, not bullies. Somehow you knew that one day you would be taking their place in the social order and this gave a sense of security.

Then we moved, my dad had a heart attack, my mom went to work, and everything changed. The only stable thing in my life was knowing that my dog, Skipper, would be there to see me when I got home, excited and eager to play. But he got hit by a car. I found him stiff by the side of the road after he'd been missing for three days. I brought him home in a shovel and buried him under my window, marked with a stone that I etched in crayon: "What the Lord giveth, the Lord taketh away."

Then, amid all this upheaval, I suddenly found myself in seventh grade—the worst year of my life up to that time. Nameless faces in endless hallways. Tough kids with taps on their shoes, toothpicks in their teeth, long black combs in their pockets for running through slicked-back hair. They'd push you aside as they passed in the halls, constantly demonstrating your rung on the social ladder. The clang-clang-clang of lockers with cryptic combinations that had to be entered precisely, perfectly—they made you late for class, even though somehow it seemed no one else was late. I *still* have anxious dreams about that.

And my glasses. ("Hey, four-eyes!")

My mother bought my clothes. The off-brand jeans didn't pass muster when all the other boys wore Levi's. And plain-colored, permanent-press, aerodynamically collared shirts were no match for Madras shirts and Oxford cloth with button-down collars. No-scuff black shoes that could double for Sunday best also were a little self-conscious next to the Bass Weejuns.

You'd think going out for football—as a quarterback, no less—would have helped make me an insider. But I was fourth-string QB (actually, *tied* for fourth string), and only because they didn't have enough linemen to make a fifth string.

I was skinny and small. I remember getting a supplement called Weight On to put in my milk, but it never seemed to work. While I tried to pump up and bulk up, those muscleman ads in the comic books never delivered. I never showered after gym, no matter how sweaty I got. Some who did shaved and had pitted faces and deep voices. I was, well, everything they weren't.

S. E. Hinton's novel *The Outsiders* illustrates the clash between the "Socs" (short for *socials*) and the "Greasers." About the latter she writes: "They grew up on the outside of society. They weren't looking for a fight. They were looking to belong." That's what we're all looking for, isn't it? To belong. Preferably somewhere that defines our identity and establishes it with a sense of security.

During those shaky years of developing adolescence we all tried to find our way inside, one way or another. Football. Cheerleading. Band. Basketball. The chess club. The school newspaper. The yearbook staff. Somewhere, anywhere—just not on the outside. We tried to find the "in" people to eat lunch with, talk with, hang out with after school. We tried to find and go to the "in" weekend parties.

Except my dad didn't much let me *go* to parties. Or wear my hair as long as the other boys. Or have my shirttail out when I left the house in the morning. My dad was a football coach. A *Texas* football coach. I can assure you, no Beatles music was allowed in *our* house. While the other kids were playing their albums on their own phonographs, I listened to what my parents chose—Glenn Miller, Lawrence Welk, swing music from the war era.

Fort Worth was then a very status-conscious community, with its *Society* newspaper section and its Junior League and its Debutante Ball. In terms of being an insider or an outsider, where you lived was a factor. So was the kind of car your family drove. The country club you were members of, or weren't. The money your family had, or didn't. All the things your culture or subculture labeled important were added up; their sum was the measure of whether *you* added up.

One weekend during the writing of this book, when I was staying with my daughter in Oklahoma City, I went to see my sister and her kids and an old friend from college in Fort Worth. As I drove south on I-35, coming into the north side of town, a flood of memories came back. Of my dad taking me to practices and games he scouted. Of his getting me a sack of hot roasted peanuts or a bag of popcorn, or afterward, a soft-serve ice cream cone. One recollection after another washed over me, from every part of the city and from every window of time in my life there.

Despite my reminiscing, in Fort Worth I was no insider. I had left after seminary and never returned, except for Thanksgiving or Christmas, an occasional wedding or funeral. Here's the odd thing: For some reason, almost as if it had a gravitational pull, the old neighborhood drew me back. Not every time, but most times.

I would drive down our street, around the corner with the light post, where we congregated in the sigh of a summer evening, watching movies at the Westerner Drive-In Theater. Past the empty lot where we played baseball, and down the street where our barber lived. To Castleberry Elementary, where, if school was out, I would get out of my car and look through the windows. I could see the cast-iron radiators that clanked as they heated up. The blackboards caked with chalk dust at the edges, the perfect cursive alphabet mounted across the top. The old wooden desks, "love" initials immortalized on them, then scratched out when that love proved mortal after all.

It was all a pleasant trip down memory lane, until . . . one day, on one of those trips, tears inexplicably spilled from my eyes.

About a year later, on a night when I was in town by myself, I stopped the car at the end of the neighborhood. As I started walking, my eyes welled up. I sat on the curb under that light post and began to sob. After a while, I tried walking again; I reached the far end of the block before the darkness hid me. Then I cried as hard as I ever had in my life.

□ □ □ ▣

In chapter 9, we'll return to my story, to what drew me home, to what made me cry.

But first, there are other stories to tell.

FOR DISCUSSION AND STUDY

1. God doesn't stop his pursuit when he brings us safely into the fold. In what way(s) have you perceived God pursuing you even after you welcomed him into your life? Is there a lost "part" of you that you sense he has been looking for?

2. How often do you feel like an outsider? Is there something that makes you think, or has you convinced, that you don't belong, at least in certain groups or settings?

3. What, or whom, have you looked to and relied on for a sense of security and constancy when everyone and everything else seemed unreliable or in upheaval?

WHOLEHEARTED THANKS

For those who, in ways they probably never realized, played a part on Jesus' behalf in pursuing me . . . finding me . . . carrying me . . . celebrating me:

Greg, Becky, Bob, The Chetter Group, The Downing House, Jerry, Martha Dell, Mary Lou, Randy, Carol, Denise, Lucky, Renee, Wanda, Tim, Anne, Albert, Steve, Gregory, Brené, Frederick, Henri, Elaine, Kimberly, Andy, Wendy, Don, Todd, Susan, Logan, Scott, Ann, Richard, Rick, Trevor, Darnell, Leslie, Robert, Archie, Jack, Leif, Charles, Bryon, Tricia, Loma Linda.

THE PURSUIT | 1

I fled Him, down the nights and down the days;
  I fled Him, down the arches of the years;
I fled Him, down the labyrinthine ways
    Of my own mind; and in the mist of tears
I hid from Him, and under running laughter.
      Up vistaed hopes I sped;
      And shot, precipitated,
Adown Titanic glooms of chasmèd fears,
  From those strong Feet that followed, followed after.
  followed after.
      But with unhurrying chase,
      And unperturbèd pace,
Deliberate speed, majestic instancy,
      They beat—and a Voice beat
      More instant than the Feet—
"All things betray thee, who betrayest Me."

              —Francis Thompson
              The Hound of Heaven

t started out as a mystery.

In February 1887, Wilfrid Meynell, editor of the Catholic literary magazine *Merry England,* received a parcel of disheveled manuscripts, smudged and rough around the edges, including this unsigned note: "In enclosing the accompanying article for your inspection, I must ask your pardon for the soiled state of the manuscript. It is due not to slovenliness, but to the strange places and circumstances under which it has been written."

His interest piqued, Meynell leafed through the unsigned papers, wondering about whoever had sent them; the return address was only a London post office box. *The Passion of Mary* was one of the poems. *Paganism Old and New* and *Dream-Tryst* were among a few other pieces of poetry and prose.

Meynell was busy getting the next month's issue ready for print, so, to place them aside for the time being, he scrolled the sheaf of papers into a pigeonhole behind his desk. Sometime later he pulled them out to read, and one poem particularly moved him. He inquired at the post office, which didn't have any helpful information. Unable to discover the person who had penned the work, he finally decided to publish it in hopes that its author would see it in the magazine and contact him.

On a spring day in 1888, shortly after the poem had been published, its author did write the editor. The return address this time was a chemist's shop. When Meynell went to inquire about the mysterious poet, the chemist told him the man was down on his luck and out in the streets, selling matches in order to live and to pay off his bill for opium he had purchased. Meynell paid the debt and wrote an invitation to meet at his office.

One day, unannounced, a tired, used-up, thirtysomething man showed up. His clothes were threadbare and stained from sleeping on London's streets. The leather in his shoes was cracked and broken. His body was frail and gaunt. The years of addiction had taken their toll.

The man introduced himself as Francis Thompson. When Meynell asked about his life, he shared his story—little by little.

Thompson had been born in 1859, into a respected, well-to-do Catholic family. He was educated at Upshaw College, where his love of literature had found fertile soil in which to thrive. After graduating, he went to Owens College to study medicine, largely at the urging of his father, himself a doctor. Medicine proved wearisome to him, though, and Thompson dropped out. An argument with his father ensued, and he left home for London. There he took a number of jobs, none of which interested him, and at last he made the streets his home. He became so destitute he wasn't even allowed in the public library.

By this time he was an addict. His drug use had started shortly after he read *Confessions of an English Opium-Eater*, a book his mother had given him on his eighteenth birthday and whose author used the drug to induce dreamlike visions that inspired his creativity. Thompson sought to do the same. He had gained easy access to drugs from his father's clinic and from medical school, and it wasn't difficult finding another supplier once he arrived in London.

Between the time he had sent his manuscripts to Meynell and one was published, the poet fell into a deep depression. In the summer of 1887, he unsuccessfully attempted suicide. Shortly after that, a prostitute befriended him. She shared her lodgings, her food, and her income. After he became published, and his life seemed on more solid footing, she disappeared one misty night, never to be heard from again. Thompson, who never revealed her name, described her in his poetry as his "saviour."

The Meynell family watched over him, placing him under a doctor's care and sending him to a monastery in Sussex, where he was temporarily freed from his addiction. He started writing poetry again, and Meynell brought him back to London, where he was introduced to friends and mentors. This was a productive time for him. Though Meynell alone realized the staggering nature of his genius, little by little his work became read and praised. He relapsed from time to time, would be sent away to another monastery for care, would always recover, but never for long.

From 1889 to 1896, Francis Thompson wrote three volumes of poetry. Between 1901 and 1904, he wrote 250 reviews and articles. His essay on Shelley was immediately received with acclaim. His most noted work, "The Hound of Heaven," was recognized then by one critic as "one of the very few great odes of which the language can boast" and hailed by another scholar as "one of the great poems, if not the greatest lyrical poem in the English language."

This autobiographical work (see complete text in the appendix) is not a poetic retelling of the parable of the prodigal son (who pursued life in a distant country, wasting his inheritance on excess), but rather about a man who sought a meaningful life apart from God—much as Solomon speaks of in Ecclesiastes, as C. S. Lewis did at Oxford, and in fact, as many of us once did and in many ways still do.

Like a hare flushed from his hiding place, he darted from one refuge to another as the Hound hotly pursued. Until at last he was cornered. Turning to face the predator, however, the man realized its true identity. It was not a hound, nor he the hare; it was God, a father, and he, his son. In the end, to that son the Father speaks:

> *All which I took from thee I did but take,*
> *Not for thy harms,*
> *But just that thou might'st seek it in My arms.*
> *All which thy child's mistake*
> *Fancies as lost, I have stored for thee at home:*
> *"Rise, clasp My hand, and come!"*
> *Halts by me that footfall:*
> *Is my gloom, after all,*
> *Shade of His hand, outstretched caressingly?*
> *"Ah, fondest, blindest, weakest,*
> *I am He Whom thou seekest!*
> *Thou dravest love from thee, who dravest Me."*

It is a reversal so startling, and a revelation so stunning, it almost takes your breath away.

Tragically, in 1907, the poet relapsed into addiction. With his condition complicated by tuberculosis, his own breath was taken away, and on November 13, at the age of forty-eight, Francis Thompson died.

□ □ □ ■

Thompson's poem, which expresses a universal truth of the human condition, has haunted readers "down the nights and down the days" . . . "down the arches of the years."

Playwright Eugene O'Neill was one of them; journalist Dorothy Day, another. David Scott writes of their entwined stories in his essay, "God, the Hound of Heaven," from which I have condensed and paraphrased in the following paragraphs.

It was 1917, on a piercing winter night in Greenwich Village. Huddled in the back room of a bar, known as the Hell Hole, was a Bohemian gathering of artists, intellectuals, and misfits. Among them were the country's premiere playwright, Eugene O'Neill, and the left-wing journalist Dorothy Day, his close friend, confidante, and drinking buddy. Maybe it was the booze, maybe because the hour was way past closing time, but O'Neill seemed unusually melancholy.

> *I fled Him, down the nights and down the days;*
> *I fled Him, down the arches of the years . . .*

He quoted the poem from memory, his words breathed into the smoke-filled room like the sigh of a footsore soul who had walked too many lonely sidewalks on too many winter nights.

> *I fled Him, down the labyrinthine ways*
> *Of my own mind; and in the mist of tears*
> *I hid from Him . . .*

Day had never heard O'Neill speak of this poem before, and it sobered her, sobered everyone. Cigarette smoke curled upward and hung in the air like wispy apparitions, looking down, listening. Haunting, the words he spoke, the way he spoke them. Everyone was hushed and still.

Shortly after leaving the Hell Hole, Day and O'Neill parted company, not to see each other again for a decade.

He wrote of a God who failed to make good on his promises, of sin and shame and the terror of death. He won four Pulitzers and the Nobel Prize in Literature, but happiness eluded him.

She married twice, conceived twice, aborted twice, and finally bore a daughter by a man she never married. In December 1927, she surrendered to the relentless pursuit of heaven's Hound and entered the Catholic Church.

She lived a life of poverty, with no income and no security, caring for the homeless on the streets not far from the Hell Hole.

She wrote of a merciful God.

Many believe the church will one day declare her a saint.

Dorothy Day never stopped praying for her friend, who had opened her eyes with the words he spoke. "It is one of those poems," she wrote in her autobiography, *From Union Square to Rome*, "that awakens the soul, recalls to it the fact that God is its destiny."

We don't know if Eugene O'Neill's soul was ever so awakened. We do know that while he lay on his deathbed in Boston in 1953, Dorothy Day was with him. She summoned a priest to his side. Keeping vigil, she prayed. She prayed he would at last unclench his fist and grasp the hand that had been reaching out to him for so many years, hoping to hear the words he recited in a barroom on that blustery winter night:

> All which I took from thee I did but take,
>   Not for thy harms,
> But just that thou might'st seek it in My arms.
>   All which thy child's mistake
> Fancies as lost, I have stored for thee at home:
>   Rise, clasp My hand, and come!

□ □ □   ▪

Poet, playwright, journalist.

Each was pursued by God, relentlessly.

John Kelman, in *Among Famous Books*, reveals Thompson's genius in how he paced his lines, which tells us something important about the pursuit.

The poem, by a strange device of rhythm, keeps up the chase in the most vividly dramatic realism. The meter throughout is irregular, and the verses swing onward for the most part in long, sweeping lines. But five times, at intervals, the sweep is interrupted by a stanza of shorter lines, varied slightly yet in essence the same—

But with unhurrying chase,
And unperturbèd pace,
Deliberate speed, majestic instancy,
They beat—and a Voice beat
More instant than the Feet—
"All things betray thee, who betrayest Me."

By this means the Hound's footfall is heard in all the pauses. In short, staccato measures we hear the movement of the feet padding after the soul from behind. It is a daring use of the onomatopoeic device in poetry, effective to a wonder, binding the whole of the ode into the unity of a single chase.

□ □ □ ■

He who inhabits eternity is not rushed for time. His chase is unhurried. His pace, unperturbed. His speed, deliberate. His feet move in other strides. He is not concerned that we outdistance him at the start or that we dart ahead and slip unseen into some thicket. His eyes are sharp. His scent, keen. His energy, tireless.

Apart from him, as the poem affirms, there is no ultimate meaning in life, either life in general or our lives in particular. Apart from him, there is no lasting fulfillment. Regardless of how many worldly prizes we accumulate, the soul is still folded over a drink in the smoky back room of some hellhole, with promises the alcohol made earlier, betraying it.

Where *can* we find love, apart from him?
Where can we find joy?
Peace?
As his feet hunt us, his voice haunts us:

> *"All things betray thee, who betrayest Me."*

FOR DISCUSSION AND STUDY

1. How do you relate to Francis Thompson's "The Hound of Heaven"? What flights have you taken from God? In what situations or circumstances have you run, and where have you gone?

2. Describe how, when you've sought recourses apart from God, you recognized the betrayal of your hope for finding fulfillment, meaning, joy, and peace in life.

3. How often have your fists been firmly and stubbornly clenched in resistance, in fear, in bitterness, in misguided ambition? As God has reached for you in pursuit, what have you found in your hands?

THE PURSUER | 2

I never felt I had much of a choice with Jesus; he was relentless. I didn't experience him so much as the hound of heaven, as the old description has it, as the alley cat of heaven, who seemed to believe that if it just keeps showing up, mewling outside your door, you'd eventually open up and give him a bowl of milk. Of course, as soon as you do, you're f——ed, and the next thing you know, he's sleeping on your bed every night, and stepping on your chest at dawn to play a little push-push.

—Anne Lamott

Anne Lamott's *Bird by Bird* is one of my favorite books on writing, and in her bracingly honest memoir, *Traveling Mercies*, she recounts her conversion. This latter has been widely read, and likely you are familiar with it. What I want you to see in it, however, is something you may not have noticed.

Should you not have read this part of her story, here is a summary:

In the spring of 1984, Lamott found herself pregnant from a relationship with a man she did not love. She did not want to have a child, let alone *his* child. A friend took her to get an abortion.

After the friend drove her home to recover, she felt such enormous sadness that its presence was almost palpable. She tried to push it away with pain pills the doctor had given her, washing them down with alcohol, drinking through the night, through the pain, through the sorrow.

One night after another she continued this ritual of remorse. By the seventh night, she noticed she was bleeding profusely. Hours later, the bleeding stopped. Exhausted, she crawled back into bed, frightened and alone and disgusted with herself. Her weakened body trembled as she turned off the light. She lay in the dark, quiet and still.

Then she felt it.

An almost encroaching presence. Someone was there, she was sure of it. She turned on the light by her bed. Nothing. Her suddenly sober eyes darted over the room. Still nothing. Finally, she turned off the light. She took shallow breaths, trying to hear the slightest sound, but there was none. She lay still and quiet, waiting.

Then she felt it. The presence had returned. Someone *was* in the room. And this time she knew who it was. It was Jesus. She felt him sitting in her bedroom loft, hunched in the corner.

Her response to such a sacred moment?

I was appalled. I thought about my life and my brilliant hilarious progressive friends, I thought about what everyone would think of me if I became a Christian, and it seemed an utterly impossible thing that simply could not be allowed to happen. I turned to the wall and said out loud, "I would rather die."

Jesus said nothing in reply. He just sat in the corner, she said, "watching me with patience and love."

She tried to shake her hangover the next morning, and she tried to shake the memory of the last night. At first she dismissed it. After all, she hadn't actually *seen* anything. Or *heard* anything. It was just a feeling or a premonition. Who knows, maybe it was alcohol-induced. Or possibly the loss of blood contributed to it.

> But then, everywhere I went, I had the feeling that a little cat was following me, wanting me to reach down and pick it up, wanting me to open the door and let it in. But I knew what would happen: you let a cat in one time, give it a little milk, and then it stays forever. So I tried to keep one step ahead of it, slamming my houseboat door when I entered or left.

The next Sunday she went back to a black church in the ghetto part of town. She had been attending lately, mostly just staying for the music. This time, though, she was too hungover even to stand during the songs. She was still sitting when they finished, and she ended up staying for the sermon. The preacher's words seemed ridiculous to her. But then, the closing song was, in her words, "so deep and pure and raw that I could not escape. . . . I felt like their voices or *something* was rocking me in its bosom, holding me like a scared kid, and I opened up to that feeling— and it washed over me."

She ducked out before the service was over, weeping as she ran. All the while she felt the presence of that little cat, padding after her. Hard to run with a hangover, though, and she slowed to a walk. She came to her houseboat, pausing at the door, her head hung in defeat. She blurted out an expletive, then sighed: "I quit. All right. You can come in."

And that, as she put it, "was my beautiful moment of conversion."

□ □ □　■

I want to put Thompson's poetic image in dialogue with another man's experience, to demonstrate how we find ways to make sense of our experience with God by using such images. If you think Thompson's imagery is harsh, take a look at the ones Jeremiah uses in Lamentations:

I'm the man who has seen trouble,
*   trouble coming from the lash of God's anger.*
He took me by the hand and walked me
*   into pitch-black darkness.*
Yes, he's given me the back of his hand
*   over and over and over again.*

He turned me into a scarecrow
*   of skin and bones, then broke the bones.*
He hemmed me in, ganged up on me,
*   poured on the trouble and hard times.*
He locked me up in deep darkness,
*   like a corpse nailed inside a coffin.*

He shuts me in so I'll never get out,
*   manacles my hands, shackles my feet.*
Even when I cry out and plead for help,
*   he locks up my prayers and throws away the key.*
He sets up blockades with quarried limestone.
*   He's got me cornered.*

He's a prowling bear tracking me down,
*   a lion in hiding ready to pounce.*
He knocked me from the path and ripped me to pieces.
*   When he finished, there was nothing left of me.*
He took out his bow and arrows
*   and used me for target practice.*

He shot me in the stomach
  with arrows from his quiver.
Everyone took me for a joke,
  made me the butt of their mocking ballads.
He forced rotten, stinking food down my throat,
  bloated me with vile drinks.

He ground my face into the gravel.
  He pounded me into the mud.
I gave up on life altogether.
  I've forgotten what the good life is like.
I said to myself, "This is it. I'm finished.
  God is a lost cause."

3:1–18

Those images best describe the feeling Jeremiah had about what he was going through. That wasn't the reality behind those images, though, any more than was it the reality that God was chasing Francis Thompson as a hound chases a hare, which is a savage pursuit that ends in the hare's brutal death.

In Thompson's poem, a moment of unveiling reveals the true identity of his pursuer. The same is true in Jeremiah's. In the very next verse, the poet's thinking takes a turn, revealing the truth:

I'll never forget the trouble, the utter lostness,
  the taste of ashes, the poison I've swallowed.
I remember it all—oh, how well I remember—
  the feeling of hitting the bottom.
But there's one other thing I remember,
  and remembering, I keep a grip on hope:

God's loyal love couldn't have run out,
  his merciful love couldn't have dried up.

They're created new every morning.
How great your faithfulness!
I'm sticking with God (I say it over and over).
He's all I've got left.

3:19–24

In a span of six stanzas, Jeremiah goes from saying "God is a lost cause" to "He's all I've got left." Which, in my own experience, rings true. I have had plenty of manic-depressive episodes when I pray, going from one extreme to another. If you read through the Psalms, you will find that same bipolar swing of emotions, often within the same prayer.

My point in placing Jeremiah's words in dialogue with Thompson's is to check whether Thompson's experience rings true. To me, it does. It also resonates with my own experience. There are times I have felt hounded by God, felt the adrenaline coursing through my veins as I fled. I've felt like prey, at times, only to discover in the end that it was not the pursuit of a predator for its prey but of a lover for its beloved.

□ □ □ ■

I want now to show how Lamott's experience differs from Thompson's, and this can be seen in their chosen descriptive images. Thompson envisions heaven's hound, while Lamott pictures heaven's alley cat. The one image is harsh and frightening; the other is soft and endearing.

Who's right?

They both are. They selected images to best describe what they felt and thought amid their respective experiences with God. As Thompson's harsher image is similar in some respects to Jeremiah's, so Lamott's softer image resembles the one Jesus uses in Luke 15:

Now all the tax-collectors and "outsiders" were crowding around to hear what he had to say. The Pharisees and the scribes complained of this, remarking, "This man accepts sinners and even eats his meals with them."

So Jesus spoke to them, using this parable: "Wouldn't any man among you who owned a hundred sheep, and lost one of them, leave the ninety-nine to themselves in the open, and go after the one which is lost until he finds it? And when he has found it, he will put it on his shoulders with great joy, and as soon as he gets home, he will call his friends and neighbours together. 'Come and celebrate with me,' he will say, 'for I have found that sheep of mine which was lost.' I tell you that it is the same in Heaven—there is more joy over one sinner whose heart is changed than over ninety-nine righteous people who have no need for repentance."

vv. 1–7 PHILLIPS

"The shepherd" is used a number of times biblically to describe the Father (e.g., Psalm 23) and the Son (e.g., John 10:11–16). A culture with Bedouin roots could hardly receive a more winsome image to describe God's relentless pursuit of the one who has strayed from the fold and now is alone and afraid.

A pursuing hound, a purring cat, a lion ready to pounce, a shepherd off to the rescue.

Seeing these different images of God as pursuer reminds me of *The Runaway Bunny*, a children's book by Margaret Wise Brown that was published in 1942 and has never gone out of print. It begins like this:

> Once there was a little bunny who wanted to run away.
> So he said to his mother, "I am running away."
> "If you run away," said his mother, "I will run after you.
> For you are my little bunny."

Turn the page, and the bunny tells his mother that if she runs after him, he will turn into a fish and swim away from her.

Turn the page, and she counters by saying that if he becomes a fish in a stream, she will become a fisherman and fish for him.

Turn again, and a two-page spread shows the mother fly-fishing with a carrot as bait, trying to catch her little bunny downstream.

You see where the story is going. Whatever he wants to become in order to flee from her, she is determined to become whatever she must in order to find him. He decides to become a rock on a high mountain, and she decides to become a climber. He decides to be a flower in a hidden garden, and she decides to become a gardener. And so it goes to the end, until the bunny finds himself exhausted trying to come up with more ideas.

"Shucks," said the bunny, "I might as well just stay where I am and be your little bunny."
And so he did.
"Have a carrot," said the mother bunny.

On the final page, they are huddled together below ground, eating carrots.

That story emulates the heart of the gospel: God's passionate pursuit of the runaway who doesn't realize how much he is loved. It is the story of humanity fleeing the One who loves us most in favor of hiding behind fig-leaf coverings and shrubs . . . on a ship to far-off Tarshish . . . in a darkened cave.

In children's book form, how might God tell the story of *The Runaway Adam and Eve . . . The Runaway Jonah . . . The Runaway Elijah*?

If you hide in the garden, I will walk through it and find you. And if you have used leaves to cover your shame, I will dress you instead with soft, warm skins.

If you flee on a ship, I will become the storm that turns it back. If it doesn't turn back, I will rock it until you are thrown overboard. And when you land in the sea, I will become the fish that swallows you so you won't drown. And then I will spit you onto the land so we can talk.

If you run away and crawl into a cave, I will become a gentle breeze that finds its way in; I will come to you, and I will whisper to you in the wind as it passes.

Here and there in the Old Testament, God or his divine envoy assumes another form. Three strangers in human veil come to Abraham with a revelation that changes the course of history. A being with supernatural strength jumps the namesake of God's people in the night, wrestling him until dawn; after being blessed, Jacob realizes he has been struggling with God.

Some scholars believe these and other events to be theophanies, appearances of the preincarnate Christ, who, having temporarily taken on human form, appears on earth in order to pursue someone here.

In the greatest form-changing event in history—the incarnation—the Son of God takes on human flesh, this time permanently, to continue the pursuit. Here is how Frederick Buechner describes that event and its ramifications:

> The child born in the night among beasts. The sweet breath and steaming dung of the beasts. And nothing is ever the same again.
>
> Those who believe in God can never in a way be sure of him again. Once they have seen him in a stable, they can never be sure where he will appear or to what lengths he will go or to what

ludicrous depths of self-humiliation he will descend in his wild pursuit of man. If holiness and the awful power and majesty of God were present in this least auspicious of all events, this birth of a peasant's child, then there is no place or time so lowly and earthbound but that holiness can be present there too. And this means that we are never safe, that there is no place where we can hide from God, no place where we are safe from his power to break in two and recreate the human heart because it is just where he seems most helpless that he is most strong, and just where we least expect him that he comes most fully.

What does all this mean to us?

It means there is no place for us to hide either.

It means we can never be sure where God will appear . . . or to what lengths he will go . . . or to what ludicrous depths of self-humiliation he will descend in his relentless pursuit of the part of us that is lost.

There is no place we are safe from his power to break our heart in order to recreate our heart. Not in the back alley of some street in London, or in the back room of some bar in Greenwich Village. Not in some houseboat in Marin County, or in some ivory tower at Oxford.

No place, however shadowed or sordid, can hide us.

It is in those places, where we least expect him, that he comes most fully.

FOR DISCUSSION AND STUDY

1. Francis Thompson envisioned God pursuing him like a hound from heaven. Anne Lamott saw God as heaven's alley cat. Jeremiah experienced God as a lion ready to pounce. Jesus portrayed God as the Good Shepherd. Why do you think God comes to us in different ways? How do you picture him in his pursuit of *you*?

2. In the children's book *The Runaway Bunny*, the mother rabbit says that no matter where her baby runs, she will go after him, assuming any form necessary in order to find him and bring him home. What are some of the "forms" the Father and Son have taken on to pursue individuals or groups? Has anyone ever pursued you in this way? If so, describe that person's behavior. If you have not experienced this, describe how your life might have been different if someone *had* pursued you relentlessly to bring you home.

3. Reread the words of Frederick Buechner (on the Incarnation) and prayerfully reflect upon them. Think of when God surprised you by showing up in a way or at a time or place where you least expected him.

THE NATURE OF THE PURSUIT | 3

You must picture me alone in that room at Magdalen, night after night, feeling, whenever my mind lifted even for a second from my work, the steady unrelenting approach of Him whom I so earnestly desired not to meet. That which I greatly feared had at last come upon me. In the Trinity Term of 1929 I gave in, and admitted that God was God, and knelt and prayed, perhaps, that night, the most dejected and reluctant convert in all England.

—C. S. Lewis
Surprised by Joy

You've probably read that quote or perhaps the book from which it came, *Surprised by Joy*, which chronicles God's relentless pursuit throughout the course of C. S. Lewis's life. If you had read the quote but not the book, here is what may surprise you—Lewis is referring not to his conversion to Christianity but to theism. He didn't come to Christ until two years later.

In this chapter I want to show the progression of God's pursuit of Lewis from his childhood through his adulthood. Pay close attention to the places where Lewis took intellectual and theological refuge and notice how God routed him from the safety of those hiding places.

☐ THE PROGRESS OF THE PURSUIT

November 29, 1898. Clive Staples Lewis was born in Belfast, Ireland. Due to an abnormality in his thumb, he had only one joint instead of two. As he grew up, this congenital defect kept him from many activities and games, like cricket, because, among other things, he couldn't throw a ball very well. So as other boys played outside, he retreated inside, where the walls of his home were lined with books of all kinds. As he cozied up with one after another, he found himself on all sorts of exotic adventures. He especially loved and was influenced by the writings of Beatrix Potter.

Lewis and his older brother, Warren—"Warnie"—played together constantly, writing and illustrating stories for their make-believe world called "Boxen," which was populated with talking animals dressed in sophisticated clothes. Reflecting on these childhood years, he once said that "at the age of seven, and eight, I was living almost entirely in my imagination; or at least that the imaginative experience of those years now seems to me more important than anything else."

The homeschooling Lewis had for the first part of his life ended when his mother died of cancer. In the same year Lewis's grandfather and uncle—his father's father and brother—also died. The result was that, as their father grieved, Lewis and his brother were left with only each other for comfort, drawing them even closer together.

September 1908. Lewis was enrolled at the very competitive Wynyard School in Watford, where Warnie was already a pupil. But Lewis was unhappy there, and his father took him out after a year and a half.

September 1910. Lewis was enrolled as a boarding student at Campbell College but was withdrawn in November after developing breathing problems.

January 1911. The boy was sent to Malvern, England, which was widely regarded as a health resort, especially for those with upper respiratory issues. He was enrolled as a student at Cherbourg House, a prep school near Malvern College, where Warren was by now a student, and Lewis remained there until June 1913. His love of fiction developed further, and he especially loved historical works like *Quo Vadis, Darkness and Dawn, The Gladiators,* and *Ben-Hur.*

It was during this time that the young Lewis abandoned his faith. The Matron of Cherbourg House was very influential on him, contributing enormously to his decision to declare himself an atheist at age fifteen. The insecurity he had experienced after his mother's death was exacerbated by going from school to school, where he faced the loneliness of being a non-athletic boy whose literary imagination was out of step with his peers.

Summer 1913. Lewis left Cherbourg House and enrolled at Malvern College, where he studied until the following June.

September 1914. Lewis was enrolled for private tutoring with W. T. Kirkpatrick and remained for two and a half years. Kirkpatrick, a former headmaster in Northern Ireland, had been a tutor of Lewis's father and also had successfully prepared his brother for admission to the Army's Royal Military Academy. Lewis, who admired Kirkpatrick all of his adult life, came to model his method of teaching.

October 12, 1916. Lewis penned his position on faith in a letter to longtime friend Arthur Greeves:

> I think that I believe in no religion. There is absolutely no proof for any of them, and from a philosophical standpoint Christianity is not even the best. All religions, i.e., all mythologies . . . are merely man's own invention. . . . In every age the educated and thinking [people] have stood outside [religion].

June 3, 1918. Lewis again wrote Greeves: "I believe in no God, least of all in one that would punish me for the 'lusts of the flesh'; but I do believe that I have in me a spirit, a chip, shall we say, of universal spirit. . . ."

1922. Lewis was twenty-four when Ireland was partitioned. Critics have suggested that this sectarian conflict in his native Belfast would lead him to adopt an ecumenical brand of Christianity that sought to unite believers instead of to divide them.

1925 to 1954. Lewis became a tutor and lecturer at Oxford. During this time he was rousted, one by one, from his ideological refuges. But he lost four different professorships while at Oxford, and so in 1954, he took the Chair of Medieval and Renaissance Literature at rival Magdalen College at Cambridge University, where he remained until 1963.

December 21, 1929. After reading John Bunyan's *Grace Abounding,* Lewis wrote: "I . . . am still finding more and more the element of truth in the old beliefs [that] I feel I cannot dismiss . . . There must be something in it; only what?" In this pre-conversion period he also wrote, "I felt as if I were a man of snow at long last beginning to melt."

The end of 1929 is when Lewis said,

> You must picture me alone in that room at Magdalen, night after night, feeling, whenever my mind lifted even for a second from my work, the steady unrelenting approach of Him whom I so earnestly desired not to meet. That which I greatly feared had at last come upon me. In the Trinity Term of 1929 I gave in, and admitted that God was God, and knelt and prayed, perhaps, that night, the most dejected and reluctant convert in all England.

January 9, 1930. In another letter to Greeves he wrote: "In spite of all my recent changes of view, I am . . . inclined to think that you can only get what you call 'Christ' out of the Gospels by . . . slurring over a great deal."

January 30, 1930. Lewis wrote to Greeves that he "attribute[d] everything to the grace of God."

March 21, 1930. Lewis wrote, to A. K. Hamilton Jenkin, that his belief system "is not precisely Christianity, though it may turn out that way in the end." He also was attending chapels at the university.

September 19, 1931. Lewis walked and talked until around four in the morning with J. R. R. Tolkien and Hugo Dyson about myth and Christianity. Dyson's main point, said Lewis, was that "Christianity works for the believer. The believer is put at peace and freed from his sins."

September 28, 1931. At age thirty-two, Lewis rode to the Whipsnade Zoo in the sidecar of Warren's motorcycle. He later made this comment: "When we set out I did not believe that Jesus Christ is the Son of God, and when we reached the zoo I did."

October 1, 1931. Lewis wrote to Greeves: "I have just passed from believing in God to definitely believing in Christ—in Christianity."

□ □ □   ◼

C. S. Lewis's path to Christ was influenced primarily by the works of two writers. The first was nineteenth-century novelist George MacDonald, whose *Phantastes* and *Lillith* Lewis read when he was nineteen. The second was G. K. Chesterton, whose *The Everlasting Man* provided a Christian theory of history that made sense to Lewis. In *Surprised by Joy* he says:

> In reading Chesterton, as in reading MacDonald, I did not know what I was letting myself in for. A young man who wishes to remain a sound Atheist cannot be too careful of his reading. God is, if I may say it, very unscrupulous.

And, if *I* may say it, relentlessly so.

Three noted others influenced Lewis along the way. His tutor, W. T. Kirkpatrick, taught him "a form of rigorous inquiry that sought objective truth through the relentless probing of an opponent's positions and definitions, a fierce and, in Kirkpatrick's hands, exaggerated version of Socratic dialogue." Owen Barfield, one of his close friends at Oxford, contributed to Lewis's acceptance of theism by forcing him into frequent debates. And J. R. R. Tolkien, a staunch Catholic, proved to be the turning point.

A look back over C. S. Lewis's life gives the distinct impression that God picked up the scent early. At the same time, the pace of the pursuit seems to have been measured, almost methodical—unhurried. In fact, hurry would have interfered, for at each out-of-the-way refuge God had experiences prepared for the young boy: books for his developing imagination to take in, adventures (as well as misadventures) to be had along the way, people to meet who would prepare him for his destiny. Clive Staples Lewis would become one of the most influential writers in all of Christendom . . . embraced by children as well as professors . . . loved by his generation and by generations to come.

No, God was not in a hurry.

His pursuit was persistent, yes.

But it was also patient.

☐ THE PURPOSE OF THE PURSUIT

After Lewis's conversion everything changed. Everything, that is, but God's pursuit. Though just as relentless, the pursuit's purpose now shifted. Whereas the goal of the first stage was capture, the goal of the second was creation. The first part was about his *coming to* Christ; the second was about his *becoming like* Christ, which he emphatically underscored in *Mere Christianity*:

> This is the whole of Christianity. There is nothing else. It is easy to get muddled about that. It is easy to think that the Church has a lot of different objects—education, building, missions, holding services. . . . The Church exists for nothing else but to draw men into Christ, to make them little Christs. If they are not doing that, all the cathedrals, clergy, missions, sermons, even the Bible itself, are simply a waste of time. God became man for no other purpose.

To go back to the biblical image, the first part of the pursuit is *search and rescue;* the second, *search and restore.* The Shepherd searches our hiding places to find us—to bring us home.

Then he searches our heart to restore us—washing out the dirt, combing out the burrs, dressing the wounds, and continuing to watch over and care for us as we grow toward maturity.

David refers to this search in Psalm 139. He begins by stating that God has searched him in the past; then, he ends with a plea for God to continue:

> Search me, O God, and know my heart;
> Try me and know my anxious thoughts;
> And see if there be any hurtful way in me,
> And lead me in the everlasting way.
>
> vv. 23–24 NASB

In this second phase, as Lewis notes, God's pursuit is as relentless as in the first:

That is why [Jesus] warned people to "count the cost" before becoming Christians. "Make no mistake," He says, "if you let me, I will make you perfect. The moment you put yourself in My hands, that is what you are in for. Nothing less, or other, than that. You have free will, and if you choose, you can push Me away. But if you do not push Me away, understand that I am going to see this job through. Whatever suffering it may cost you in your earthly life, whatever inconceivable purification it may cost you after death, whatever it costs Me, I will never rest, nor let you rest, until you are literally perfect—until my Father can say without reservation that He is well pleased with you, as He said He was well pleased with me. This I can do and will do. But I will not do anything less."

And, as someone once said:

"God loves us as we are, but he loves us too much to leave us that way."

□ □ □ ■

I suspect if you took time to look over your shoulder and jot down dates or times when your life began to change course— dates or times tied to people and places and influences—you would see a pattern of pursuit . . .

> *with unhurrying chase,*
> *And unperturbèd pace,*

Regarding the pursuit, I also suspect you'd see a *"deliberate speed"* that's both progressive and, in the end, purposeful. I know *I* did when I looked back. I never really took time, though, until an editor asked if I'd consider writing about my life and the influences that led me to become a writer.

Her idea seemed well-intentioned but hopelessly misguided. I couldn't understand why she, anyone at the publishing house, or anyone *anywhere* would be interested. I had written about a set of twins, one of which was handicapped. About Jesus. About a baseball player. But not about me.

I had put together a small scrapbook of memories when my dad died, but nobody seemed much interested in it. After a short season on the shelf, bookstores started returning it. It almost hyperventilated in its rush to go out of print, and I resolved "never to do *that* again."

Despite that resolution, however, I called the editor back about a month later and agreed. I still didn't think anyone would be much interested; I did feel it would be a good exercise for me to go over the terrain I had traveled in order to get some perspective and to consider where God was in it all.

This experience would produce one epiphany after another and culminate in the book *Windows of the Soul*. And I did in fact discover where God was: He was in it every step of the way. For the first time I understood why Frederick Buechner called our lives, each of our lives, a "sacred journey."

I saw, for example, how God had prepared me. How he had given me skilled English teachers so that grammar and syntax were never a problem. How he had given me resonantly voiced teachers who read to me after recess, drawing me into worlds where stories lived and adventures were had and all sorts of fascinating characters introduced themselves. How he had placed me in school at a time when handwriting was taught, when your hand held a fountain pen with liquid blue ink that flowed so smoothly over paper, when writing could be sentient and addictive to where you practiced so you could see how your name looked in your best cursive.

Further, I saw how God had put me in a neighborhood that fueled my imagination . . . from unfettered freedom on the banks of the Trinity River . . . to the companionable silence of the River Oaks Library . . . to the bookshelf-bed stack of comics and Hardy Boys mysteries I read at night by flashlight . . . to the Saturday matinees at the theater . . . to the forts we made and the battles we fought from yard to yard, dodging staccato machine-gun fire to hurl grenades only to be shot through by the enemy and writhe histrionically on the ground until we were "goners."

□ □ □ ■

My childhood was something of a cross between *The Sandlot* and *Stand by Me,* without cigarette-behind-the-ear, switchblade-in-the-pocket bullies. It wasn't Mayberry, where all was basically calm and where even conflicts were amiably reasoned out and resolved. There was pain, and shame, and anger, and I then kept these inside all the way up until they started spewing out like a shaken and suddenly opened can of soda.

Nothing terrible happened to me, growing up. And for that I am grateful. But I was a sensitive kid, like Will, *Stand by Me*'s young writer. Remember how he responded to finding the dead body, compared to how the other boys did? For some reason, like him, I felt deeply about things, more deeply than the rest of the boys and even the girls I knew.

Though the three of us kids were raised in the same house, in a way we lived in three different homes, as all of us do. Something traumatic or momentous happens when one is nine, the other is six, and the other is three, and even if they all experience the same thing, they experience it in different ways, according to age, temperament, particular vantage point, and more. We are never dealing with reality when sifting through childhood memories but rather with perceptions of reality, which always have attached and interwoven emotions that in some way or another color the experience—sometimes too lightly, sometimes too darkly, and almost always distorting.

I never really understood my own hardwiring until I read Elaine Aron's *The Highly Sensitive Person*. I realized not only who I am but likewise what the gift of writing is. I no longer think it is a facility for words, or an active imagination, that makes one a writer. I don't even think it is a way of seeing the world uniquely. I have rather come to believe that it is a way of feeling: things move you, deeply, and then you feel as if every cell in your body must pay attention to what is moving you, with a sense of something like urgency. People like this grope to find something to express the feeling—a pen, a brush, a keyboard . . .

And that is how art is made. Not always, but often.

□ □ □ ■

For reasons we kids couldn't understand, we moved, quite suddenly, from the old neighborhood. Our new place was just over a mile away but also a whole school district away, so it might as well have been to another country. Again, while we couldn't know why, we never went back. Even though it was within walking distance.

Then my dad, a relatively young man in good shape, had a near-fatal heart attack and spent a month in intensive care, teetering between life and death. My mother went to work. My sister, who was in high school, worked, too. My brother was in elementary school, and I'm not sure how he fared because the truth is I wasn't a very good big brother. My dog, Skipper, was the one I mostly talked to, until the day he tried to cross a street in traffic.

So many things seemed taken, almost ripped, from my hands during that time. I filled those hands with a basketball. I remember shooting baskets after dinner until dark at the elementary school, walking there alone, practicing alone, walking home alone. The bounce of the ball off the asphalt had a peaceful rhythm that made me feel less lonely, less anxious.

Before I knew it, I found myself in W. C. Stripling Junior High, where some of the boys *were* bullies who *did* have cigarettes behind their ears and switchblades in their pockets.

Somehow all of that contributed to my becoming a writer. I had become a more inward person in response to the feelings of abandonment I experienced. In the family's move from the old neighborhood, a lot of the ground that once seemed so solidly under my feet had shifted.

Then came the onslaught of puberty with all its ongoing changes inside and out. My body went through a growth spurt, late-coming but a mercy nonetheless. From seventh grade to eighth I was surprised by how much I had grown. I remember that during a summer game of pickup football, the other players had been surprised too.

That year I went from trying out for quarterback, which had been my dad's suggestion, to trying out for end, where I played through ninth grade until I hurt my knee against a team of what looked like chain-gang criminals. I still remember the face of the guy, pitted with acne, who ran past my writhing body down the sidelines for a touchdown.

After surgery to remove some cartilage in my knee, I just played basketball. The one good thing that came out of this was that the cheerleaders started paying more attention to me, asking how I was doing, grimacing empathetically when I answered, patting me on the shoulder, telling me to hang in there, smiling at me. I developed crushes on all of them.

High school was better. I found ways to thin what seemed to me a forest of hair between my eyebrows. I discovered deodorant and men's cologne. I bought all my own clothes. I was still self-conscious with girls but found that being funny made it easier to be around them and seemed to mildly endear them to me. Some anyway. A few. Okay, two. I'm sure there were two. One I even dated.

One day, during my junior year, a Young Life leader came around and worked his way into a pickup game. Then he kept showing up, working his way into our lives. I went to camp that summer, and it was, as he promised, the best week of my life. The summer after graduating I went with him to a college prep camp, where, after "the Cross talk," I gave what little I knew of my life to what little I knew of Jesus. I remember sitting next to a tree under a star-speckled Colorado sky, deeply touched at all Jesus had gone through to find me and carry me home. I remember thanking him and saying, "I don't know if you would ever need me for anything, but if you ever did, I would be happy to help." Or something like that. Little did I know he would take me up on the offer.

In elementary school I had wanted to be an oceanographer. The library books I checked out had pictures of sharks and coral reefs and a mysteriously kelpy undersea world. Watching *Sea Hunt* had something to do with it too.

In high school, after a canoe trip in Canada with the Boy Scouts, I wanted to be a forest ranger.

In college I was a radio/TV/film major and wanted to make films. Friday nights at the drive-in, Saturday matinees at the River Oaks Theater, and *All Night Movies* on Channel 8 had something to do with that.

The two most influential art forms for me have been books and film. My mother had read me stories; my father had told me stories. And I had teachers who read in class, and those influences had a lasting impact. The library merely fanned an already lit flame for story. So did the neighborhood theater.

During the spring of my senior year I had narrowed my college options. The University of Texas in Austin was my first choice. Texas Christian University in my hometown of Fort Worth was second. I'd been accepted to both, but only TCU had a room for me in their dorms; UT's were full, and, if I enrolled, I would have to stay off campus.

So one rainy morning, my father, mother, and I headed to Austin. We were barely on the road when the car hydroplaned in a turn, spinning us around repeatedly. Fortunately there were no oncoming cars, and we didn't hit anything. After we came to a stop, Mom felt this was a bad sign, that maybe God was telling us not to go and that we should return home. We did.

That decision was a turning point in ways I am only now beginning to understand.

I ended up at TCU, in a room they had ready for me. I began meeting friends whose significant impact on my life I would not realize for decades. Getting involved with Young Life leadership was instrumental in grounding me in my faith.

Attending McKinney Memorial Bible Church also contributed to my growth. At the time, the church didn't have a pastor; professors from Dallas Theological Seminary usually came to preach. Dallas specialized in expository preaching, which was life-changing for a kid who'd grown up Lutheran—I had never heard it before.

It wasn't long before several of us started driving to Believer's Chapel in Dallas to hear S. Lewis Johnson, head of the seminary's Greek department. Halfway through college, several of us would take a day off now and then, drive to the seminary, and sit in on classes. Gradually, one after another of my peer group applied to attend. I followed.

At the time I wasn't sure what I wanted to do with my life. Of course I was asked, on the ream of to-be-filled-out forms, but, kind of like in college, I checked the "undeclared" box and got a pass on the question for at least another year. I heard a lot of students talk about being called to the pastorate or the mission field or some other form of service, but I felt none of those. I just loved learning. A number of my friends were going to work with Young Life after graduating. I suspect I might have as well, except for one thing.

My knee, the one I'd had surgery on, was getting worse. I went to an orthopedic surgeon my second year, and he said I would have to stop the sport that had brought me so much joy for much of my life and had given me my identity for so long. I'd been taking guys to play basketball and handball, the way my own Young Life leader had done, and this was a great way to do "contact work"—it had given me, a somewhat shy person, an entry into their lives and a degree of credibility.

I still could jog on soft surfaces, the doctor told me, swim and ride a bicycle, but that was about it. After all, he said, that knee has to last the rest of your life. I drove back to seminary so depressed I skipped afternoon classes. I felt I had just returned from the death of a friend.

A part of my life was over. I couldn't do Young Life work anymore, I was sure of that. Mistakenly sure, but sure. Sports had been a bridge for me, and now that bridge was washed out. Which made me feel as though I was washed up.

Eventually I did accept the specialist's decree and began considering other options. Teaching, perhaps. In college, perhaps. But teaching what? English? Literature? I wasn't sure. After graduating with a master of theology, I started sending out résumés and immediately came to an abrasive rub with the reality that my four years of seminary didn't add up to much in secular academia. Everyone said I needed a PhD just to get a decent interview.

Which meant three more years of investment.

□ □ □　■

I had commuted daily from Fort Worth to Dallas; I had been married by the beginning of my second year at DTS and had a child by the beginning of my third year. I had worked two jobs most of that time—Young Life student staff, waiting tables, assembly line at General Motors, remodeling a house—and I was tired.

While applying for jobs, I was also teaching a Sunday school class at McKinney Memorial, where three couples asked if I would start a church in their small hometown of Aledo, just outside Fort Worth. My wife and I loved the couples; we said yes. Starting to get a regular paycheck with benefits felt really, really good.

During that time I had an itch I felt needed scratching or I might regret it someday. I felt I should give writing a try, and so I wrote my first book, a story about a set of ten-year-old twins, a boy and a girl; the boy had a mild mental and physical handicap. Finishing the novel was like finding a piece of me that had always been missing. I wept when the main character died, and I think it was those tears that told me *this is what I should be doing with my life.*

Since I had no background in writing, I spent a couple years in the business world before moving the family to East Texas. I started writing; I wrote as long as there was money to do it, and when the money ran out I went to work painting and hanging wallpaper. We sold our house, moved, and lived off the equity for another year. I was trying to make sense of where God was in all of this, if he was in it then or ever was. My only spiritual nourishment during that time was provided by my brother, who had passed on to me Chuck Swindoll sermon tapes.

I ended up calling Swindoll's church and sending them my résumé; they directed me to Insight for Living, which, it turned out, was as desperate to find a writer as this writer was to be found. During my years at this ministry, I learned how to edit, how to do professional work, how to meet deadlines. This gave me not only the stability but also the self-esteem I needed—mine had all but eroded.

Our years in Southern California were great times for me, personally and professionally, and for our family. I attended as many film and screenwriting classes as I could. Any education I ever had in writing, I received there.

I felt *led*, strongly led or strongly pursued, as if God were moving me toward a future that, though uncertain to me, was not uncertain to him. Along the way I learned some important truths, picked up essential skills, and met inspiring role models. I made some good friends, found an agent, and started my life as a writer.

Life was good there.

I thought it would last forever.

FOR DISCUSSION AND STUDY

1. Think back on how God has been preparing you to become the you he created you to be and to share his love with others. In retrospect, what can you identify as some of the things he specifically wanted you to experience along the way? (For example, adventures and misadventures with their accompanying lessons; people who would impact the shape of your beliefs and choices; events or interactions that for you were momentous; inspirations and ideas that would seize and stretch your imagination; artistic creations—books, paintings, films, songs, and so on—that would ignite your passion and energize your pursuits.)

2. C. S. Lewis noted that, ultimately, the church's sole purpose is to draw people to Jesus, to make them like Christ, and that God became man for this purpose alone. If *after* God has retrieved and rescued us he seeks to recreate and restore us, why do we so often think we ought to be completely different people at the moment we place our faith in him? How can this belief, in the church, contribute to people feeling like "outsiders" just for being genuine or speaking honestly?

3. Lewis also reminded us of Christ's admonition to consider what we're signing up for when we give him our lives (e.g., see Luke 14:28–33). Is there any part of you that deep down you've wanted to keep to yourself, off-limits to God? Perhaps something you've believed he might not even want to pursue—something that couldn't be rescued, wouldn't be redeemed?

4. Take some time to consider the pattern of God's pursuit, over time, in your life. What can you see that's unhurried and deliberate, both progressive and purposeful?

THE PART OF US THAT IS LOST

4

Our lives are a collection of stories—truths about who we are, what we believe, what we come from, how we struggle, and how we are strong. When we can let go of what people think, and own our story, we gain access to our worthiness—the feeling that we are enough just as we are, and that we are worthy of love and belonging. If we spend a lifetime trying to distance ourselves from the parts of our lives that don't fit with who we think we're supposed to be, we stand outside of our story and have to hustle for our worthiness by constantly performing, perfecting, pleasing, and proving.

—Brené Brown
The Hustle for Worthiness

Brené Brown is a research professor at the University of Houston Graduate College of Social Work. Her topics of study include vulnerability, courage, authenticity, and shame. Her work, which has been featured on PBS, NPR, and CNN, has led her to a concept she describes as "wholeheartedness." I want to pick up on the last part of that quote from her:

If we spend a lifetime trying to distance ourselves from the parts of our lives that don't fit with who we think we're supposed to be, we stand outside of our story and have to hustle for our worthiness by constantly performing, perfecting, pleasing, and proving.

For most of my life I *had* stood outside my story, distanced from the parts of me that didn't fit with who I thought I was supposed to be. I never realized it, of course. Now that I'm older I see it. *How did I get there, on the outside?* It was one of the questions the adult in me was now asking.

I have come to realize after a lot of counseling, a lot of reading, and a lot of conversations, that shame had a lot to do with it. Brown defines shame, in *The Gifts of Imperfection*, as the "intensely painful feeling or experience of believing that we are flawed and therefore unworthy of love and belonging." It works like "the zoom lens on a camera," she writes. "When we are feeling shame, the camera is zoomed in tight and all we see is our flawed selves, alone and struggling."

Put a makeup mirror to your face and turn on its fluorescent light. Look at the pores on your nose and the hairs in your nostrils. Focus on the wrinkles around your eyes and the gullies under them. Shame believes that this magnified face is your true face, the one everybody else—especially God—is focused on.

Shame can isolate you, drive you away from community. Shame accuses you of being unworthy of love and belonging and joy. Shame can even blackmail you. *If everyone knew the truth about you, they would see you for the fraud you are and wouldn't want to be around you.*

Here is Brown's most sobering conclusion: "Shame corrodes the very part of us that believes we are capable of change." In other words, it is a lynchpin lie. It's the deception that, if believed, will keep any change from taking place in your life. After all, if we are incapable of change, why even try?

If you're a person who believes that lie, what do you do? You hide. You hide from God, from yourself, from others. And if you *are* around others, you hide in other ways.

I used humor—that's one way I hid. I also distanced myself from the shame and anger inside.

I was in elementary school before I stopped wetting the bed, and that was a real source of shame. I would wake up at night, feel the clammy wet sheets, then hurry to put them in the washer before anyone found out. If I had time in the morning, I would shower. But sometimes I didn't have time. Once, while I was putting my things in my locker at the back of the classroom, a girl sniffed the air with disgust. "Do you *smell* that?"

I lied.

I closed my locker and slunk over to my seat. *If she smelled it,* I thought, *everyone could.*

That was a bad day in elementary school. But it was nothing compared to The Bad Year. Fifth grade. "The year of the wart."

Over a hundred of them, actually. They were like a biblical swarm of locusts—on my hands, my fingers, my cuticles. One day at recess, as we held hands to form a circle for dodge ball, the girl on my right recoiled and pulled away, looking like she had stuck her hand into fresh dog poop. She did manage to find words that matched her revulsion.

"Just say to them," my mother suggested with resolve, " 'Sticks and stones may break my bones, but words will never hurt me.' " Mom said a lot of things to me that were good and true, but this was not one of them.

The words did hurt. And they kept hurting. Everywhere I went I carried the hurt. An abscess of anger attached to it some of the time. A subterranean shame ran through me *all* of the time.

□ □ □ ▪

I recall, years later, having read the Greek philosopher Bion of Borysthenes, and the truth of his words makes me pause and reflect on my childhood: "Though boys throw stones at frogs in sport, the frogs do not die in sport but in earnest."

This thought was particularly poignant to me because as a young boy I spent so many lazy summer days at the Trinity River's West Fork, before the Army's Corps of Engineers tamed its occasional flooding with levees. I loved picking up flat rocks and whipping them across the water, counting the skips, attempting to best myself with each successive throw. Whenever I saw a frog jump from the banks and kick its way across the water, I would take aim and try to hit it. Whenever I did, I congratulated myself.

It was like a video game to me, and though I felt compassion for suffering mammals, I had never felt that way toward fish or frogs. Bion's statement changed me. I realized that what had been sport to me had inflicted wounds, sometimes fatal wounds, on a frog that was . . . just being a frog.

Then I thought about all the people I had thrown rocks at, in sport, over the years, and how adept I'd become at it. Sarcasm, intended in good humor, was what I used to keep anyone from "throwing rocks" at me first.

When I started working with Young Life, all my peers had quick tongues. They weren't mean-spirited; they were just sharp-witted. I found I loved the verbal sparring. Until, of course, those times when I had no retort. When someone else's rock hit its mark and left me momentarily stunned.

To keep that from happening, I started buying books like *1001 Insults* and *Comebacks for All Occasions*. Then, *1001 More Insults*. And more after that. I started keeping a notebook of comebacks, insults, and witticisms. If I heard anything good on TV, I would write it down. If I read anything really funny in the newspaper, I would write it down. I read these over and over until I had them memorized.

I kept the notebook in the car and read it before doing contact work, where you go to the high school for lunch or for a game to progressively "win the right to be heard." The point was getting to know kids well enough that they would come to like you, trust you, and see that you were interested in their world and their life. The bridges built through "relational evangelism" meant that when you talked about the gospel at club meetings, they listened.

When I took one of the guys from my club to play handball, he saw my notebook next to me and asked about it. And you'd have thought it was a *Playboy* magazine for how embarrassed I was. Before I could toss it into the backseat, he picked it up and started reading. Then he laughed, which made me feel better. "This is great!" he said. "Can I take it home with me?"

The following Monday I went to the school for lunch and saw him at a table, surrounded by friends who roared at the lines when he read them. He was the center of attention, and I'm sure that felt good. When he saw me and waved me over, *I* was the center of attention, and, honestly, it did feel good. It felt good not to feel so much like an outsider. It felt good to be called over and told the jokes were great, that the notebook was cool.

When I left, I took the notebook and put it beside me in the car. On the long drive back to my dorm I could feel my face flushing. Young Life is a great ministry, with a great mission: to go after the lost sheep. To the sheep I found, I was to be the best shepherd a college sophomore could be.

But I had not been a shepherd, let alone a good one; I had been a standup comic.

And it wasn't the gospel they were devouring; it was a notebook of putdowns and smack-downs and insults for all occasions.

The indicting conclusion I reached was that they didn't want to be like Jesus; they wanted to be like me.

The humor that hid me also revealed me.

What it revealed broke my heart.

□ □ □ ▪

I've thought a lot about the parable of the lost sheep since starting this book. Here it is again so you can think about it too.

> Now all the tax-collectors and "outsiders" were crowding around to hear what he had to say. The Pharisees and the scribes complained of this, remarking, "This man accepts sinners and even eats his meals with them."
>
> So Jesus spoke to them, using this parable: "Wouldn't any man among you who owned a hundred sheep, and lost one of them, leave the ninety-nine to themselves in the open, and go after the one which is lost until he finds it? And when he has found it, he will put it on his shoulders with great joy, and as soon as he gets home, he will call his friends and neighbours together. 'Come and celebrate with me,' he will say, 'for I have found that sheep of mine which was lost.' I tell you that it is the same in Heaven—there is more joy over one sinner whose heart

is changed than over ninety-nine righteous people who have no need for repentance."

Luke 15:1–7 PHILLIPS

I have had a hard time understanding why the shepherd would leave the ninety-nine that were safe for the one that wasn't.

Think through this with me. If we owned a business, how much would it affect our balance sheet if 1 percent of our inventory was lost? Whether from damage, spoilage, obsolescence, or theft, the loss is still 1 percent regardless.

How much bottom-line difference would it make to face a 1 percent write-off?

True, it has worth—1 percent isn't zero. But would it not seem vastly more prudent for us to watch over the secured 99 percent and write off the fraction we may not be able to recover? Protect the vast majority of our assets and we cap our minimal loss. Or, chase that 1 percent and risk losing everything. How could that not be needlessly reckless? How could we justify not sticking close to those who already belong to us and depend on us?

Consider this question in terms of people. By going after one, we would be leaving the ninety-nine to themselves, lacking supervision, in the open, without protection. Forging ahead alone, they could stray, fall into a pit, break a leg, or be attacked. A pack of predators could descend and scatter them in all directions.

Correct me if I'm wrong, but *who does that?*

Another hard-to-fathom factor is the length to which the shepherd would go in order to find the lost sheep. In the story, Jesus said he searched *until* he found it. Which is to say, the shepherd did not give up.

Would darkness deter him? A scornful sun, a sudden storm? Wild animals? Robbers? The treachery of the terrain?

None of these things would dissuade him.

Why?

For the one lamb that was separated from him . . . the one that was lost . . . alone . . . in danger . . . terrified—perhaps it picked up the scent of a wolf . . . or heard the howls of coyotes . . . or felt ripped by the biting wind and the piercing rain . . . or was snake-bit and swelling . . . or had tumbled down a ravine—for that one, the shepherd went to the edge, and beyond.

Why would he go to such extremes?

He goes after the sheep because it's his. He owns it and knows it. He was there at its birth, bringing it into the world. He has watched it grow up; he smiled at its wobbly attempts to walk, laughed at it gamboling all over the pasture with the other lambs. He has named it, talked with it, cared for it.

For all those reasons.

Most of all, though, because he loves it.

How much?

Enough to sacrifice his life for it, according to the story Jesus tells in John 10.

Seriously? For a sheep? *One* sheep?

We must understand this from the start. If we're going to flee God, it's going to end up like the story of *The Runaway Bunny*. He is going to find us and bring us home. Jesus suggests the shepherd drapes the lamb around his neck, almost like a shawl, one hand holding its front legs, the other holding its back ones. On the return trip, what do you think the shepherd is doing all the while? Scolding the wayward sheep? Lecturing it for not paying attention? Yelling at the top of his lungs?

See if you can answer those questions from what Jesus reveals about the relationship of the shepherd to his sheep.

> I am the Good Shepherd. The Good Shepherd puts the sheep before himself, sacrifices himself if necessary. A hired man is not a real shepherd. The sheep mean nothing to him. He sees a wolf come and runs for it, leaving the sheep to be ravaged and scattered by the wolf. He's only in it for the money. The sheep don't matter to him.
>
> I am the Good Shepherd. I know my own sheep and my own sheep know me. In the same way, the Father knows me and I know the Father. I put the sheep before myself, sacrificing myself if necessary.
>
> John 10:11–14

The Shepherd is described as good (the Greek word can also be translated "beautiful"), as having an intimate knowledge of his sheep and they of him, and as one who puts their welfare before his own, to the extent that he is even willing to give his life so they might live.

If you are still unsure about what kind of interaction such a shepherd is having with his rescued lamb, look again at Luke 15: "When he has found it, he will put it on his shoulders *with great joy*" (v. 5, emphasis added). This tells us everything we need to know. Now we can imagine the conversation—the words, the tone, the laughter, maybe even the singing.

How do you think this trembling sheep is feeling on the shepherd's shoulders, sensing the strength of his hands, hearing his familiar voice?

Notice what the shepherd does when he returns. Does he drop the sheep into a pen or plop it down amid the flock, then go about his business?

No. Either he hollers up and down the streets or goes door to door, the sheep likely still on his shoulders. Then what? He invites everybody to his house. All of them. Why? To *celebrate*. And who is the guest of honor? The newfound sheep. He's right there in the middle of it all, smack-dab in the center of the joy. Envision the scene. Everyone rubbing its wool, tousling its head, hugging its neck. Feeding it from the table, because, of course, he's famished.

Probably he's dirty and matted and perhaps even bloody from the ordeal. What would a good shepherd do about that? The happy little lamb was probably washed and combed and his wounds bound up. Probably he spent the night inside, drying off and warming up. Where did he sleep, do you think? Wherever the shepherd slept. Right next to him, likely, perhaps nuzzling his shepherd's neck before drifting off to sleep.

Here's the most beautiful thing: All this effort on the shepherd's part, all this tenderness, all this joy, and for whom? Look again at how J. B. Phillips renders Luke 15:1: "All the tax-collectors and 'outsiders' were crowding around to hear what he had to say."

It was for those who, for whatever reason, were outcasts.

□ □ □ ■

The Dictionary of Biblical Imagery explains the protocol of the meal in Jewish culture at that time.

> The meal became a place where Jews "drew the line" between insiders and outsiders in their families, communities and ethnic groups. Gentiles and strangers either were excluded or had to undergo special ritual cleansing in order to participate in even ordinary meals.

The crowd Jesus is eating with has one thing in common. They're all outsiders—tax collectors, prostitutes, petty thieves, publicans, debtors, tanners, half-breeds, misfits, foreigners— shunned by the holy huddle of the self-righteous. Gatekeepers were checking their stories to see how "she" got there or "he" got there. "Hey, this one just wandered off, looking for food, and got lost. Not a *moral* problem really—he's okay. Let him back in." Or, "Wait a minute. Her story doesn't wash; I'm not buying it. Send her packing."

Here's the point: To Jesus, it didn't matter how they had ended up on the outside. It was enough that they were out there, lost in their own way, alone in their own way, afraid in their own way. Each bore the shame of their status in the eyes of the community. And each was covering it up by huddling with other outsiders.

Think about this. What if you were the lost one. What if you were the *only* one who was lost. The following question is perhaps the one question that matters. How you answer it will go a long way toward your understanding of your self-worth: Would Jesus write off the loss your life had become?

What *would* it take for Jesus to write you off?

Well . . .

Which leper did he turn away?

Which whore did he pelt with stones?

Which blind man did he ignore?

Which thief, when he called out to be remembered?

How many demons would you have to have before he scratched your name off his list?

One? Seven? A legion?

Do you know what he did for you? He searched for you, he found you, and he brought you home.

Do you know what he does to find the part of you that is lost? The very same thing: He searches for it, finds it, brings it home. And he does this time and again, day or night, rain or shine. He searches *until he finds it*. And finding it fills him with joy.

Great joy.

For all of us who have a "part" living outside this joy, that is good news.

No. It's *great* news!

Regardless of why that part of us strays—whether it's a part that fondles a lustful thought, or aids and abets an angry feeling, or clings to unforgiveness with a clenched fist—the Shepherd leaves the 99 percent of our heart that is near him and searches for the 1 percent that isn't.

The search may last through the night or through a lifetime. But the pursuit remains relentless, and God won't give up until that part of us is found and brought home.

Shame is a far place from home, every bit as far as the distant country was from the home of the prodigal. In us there is, perhaps, a woman at the well, filled with shame, getting water outside the city so the other women won't see her and shun her. And all she wants is to be found out there, loved out there, and carried home.

There is in us, perhaps, a thief on some cross with a squandered life, and all he wants is to be remembered, and if the word he's heard is true, to be shown mercy and brought inside.

There is inside us, perhaps, a boy with epilepsy, stared at for his seizures, or a man with leprosy, scorned for his uncleanness. And all they want is to be free from the gawking and the ridicule, to be brought home where they are accepted, and though it's beyond their ability to imagine, to be celebrated.

There is a part of us, perhaps, that is paralyzed, or a part that is demonized. There is a part that is humiliated, or a part that is isolated. And those parts want only to be reunited with the rest of us—with everything that is healthy and whole.

All of us at some time or another have wandered away from our best self, gotten disoriented, become lost, and found ourselves on the outside. Our greatest need as humans is to know that we are loved, even out there, regardless of how we got there. Every Christmas we are reminded of this by the most amazing search-and-rescue mission ever launched. No carol celebrates its truth more robustly than "O Holy Night," especially the stanza

> Long lay the world
> in sin and error pining,
> till He appeared
> and the soul felt its worth.

Can *your* soul feel its worth?

By leaving the host of heaven and coming to earth that one holy night, the Good Shepherd was saying to each of us: "You are loved. You are worthy of my pursuit. Worthy to be rescued. Worthy to be carried on my shoulders, to be rejoiced over all the way home. And worthy to be celebrated in heaven by the whole neighborhood.

"You are enough *for me*.

"I hope that is enough *for you*."

□ □ □　■

It wasn't.

It should have been, but it wasn't.

I had never grasped the fullness of that holiest of nights, what it meant to the world, what it meant to me. I *should* have felt my worth. Down to the deepest part of my soul, I should have felt it. But I didn't. As I look back, my life seems to have been, to use Brown's words, a hustle for worthiness by constantly performing, perfecting, pleasing, and proving.

Much of that was for my dad.

Dad came from a simple, working-class neighborhood in Pittsburgh, Kansas. His mother, Theodocia, died when he was four. She was an angel, from what he remembers of her, from what the neighbors kept telling him about her after she passed, from the memories his father shared with him. His father, Ben, a barber and lay preacher in the Baptist church, succumbed to alcohol after Theo died. Eventually he married his housekeeper, but he was never the same. And my dad knew it, even at four years old.

Dad, the youngest in the family, mostly raised himself. He grew up a freckled-faced redhead; he also was prone to bed-wetting, and was picked on by the older boys in the neighborhood. He often came home bloodied and crying, until one day his dad told him that if he ever came home crying from a fight again, he could look forward to another beating, from him.

That was the last time he came home crying. He pretty much fought his way through the subsequent years—the growing-up years, pool hall years, football years, army years. Still, he was never one to pick a fight. And he would always take up for the underdog.

He had a tender heart, but at the same time he could get really angry, really fast. I remember thinking a blood vessel might break in his neck. I never got a spanking I didn't deserve, yet spanking seemed not so much a last resort as the first and only resort. He used a switch, most of the time, and I was terrified of it. I'm sure his discipline was lighter than he got from his father, just as my discipline was lighter on my children than I got. Dad never intentionally shamed me, but a lot of shame came to me through that switch he kept beside our refrigerator.

One summer he took a job driving oil tankers in New Mexico. Mom and us kids stayed with Grandma and Grandpa in what seemed then a gigantic house with an equally gigantic yard in the shady, manicured suburb of Elmhurst, Illinois. I still have some of the letters Dad wrote reminding me to be a good boy and telling me I would have to be the man of the house now. Though I was never sure what this meant, I somehow felt it had something to do with putting my toys away and standing up straight with my face wiped clean, my shirttail tucked in, and helping out more. I felt he needed me to be that boy, and for some important reason I felt the family needed me to be that man.

Because of heart problems, Dad walked a lot at night after work, and I often walked with him. He loved to tell stories, and I loved to listen, so we made good walking partners. He told stories of his old neighborhood during the Depression, where everyone looked out for one another, helped each other in sickness and in death. He told about everybody washing clothes on the same day, each house brewing a vat of hot, soapy water, heated by a fire of chopped wood. He recalled how his mom had stirred the clothes with a wooden paddle, wrung them out, and hung them on the clothesline.

He told me how they made their own bar soap. He told me how hard his mom worked, washing and ironing, cooking and canning, keeping house, keeping up with the kids. She never raised her voice, he said on a number of occasions, and never got angry. If he sassed her, she'd just wait until Ben got home. After supper, Papa—as my dad called him—would read the family Bible and then put it aside, lower his reading glasses, and peer down the table at his wife. "Anything I need to know, Theo?" And that's when one of the kids might get taken to the woodshed.

On those long walks down our lamp-lit streets, he also told me stories of Halloween pranks they used to pull, like tipping over outhouses or putting a sack of dog poop on a porch, lighting it on fire, then knocking on the door and running for a place to hide so they could watch someone frantically stomp on it. He spoke of home remedies and how they always made do; how his dad bought the neighborhood's first radio and put it on the porch at night so anyone who wanted could come and listen to *The Green Lantern* or *Lights Out*.

He told of the games they played, from "Kick the Can" to "Go, Sheepy, Go"; he recalled events with such evocative detail that if we turned at the corner and headed out of our neighborhood, it wouldn't have surprised me if I found myself walking into *his*.

He told of his coaching years too, and of the war, though without the gore. It seemed like such an adventure that years later I almost volunteered for Vietnam. Dad talked me out of that and into college instead.

□ □ □ ■

Dad's presence loomed large in my life, and I found myself wanting to please, to perform, to make good for him and for the family, to make them all proud. I was "a Gire," after all, and he always added, "and that's somethin'."

While it was clear I had something to live up to, it wasn't so clear to me at the time what that was.

My dad had dedicated a big part of his life to the game of football, so I knew it was something that mattered to him. He still watched it on television. Still drew X's and O's to map out plays. Still had former players drop by, introducing their wives or kids to him.

At Dad's suggestion, I went out for football and tried out for quarterback, though I couldn't throw a spiral, and if I ever did it was a quirk of statistical odds.

I kept a notebook of ideas and quotes and other things to say, because he thought it would help me if I were ever called upon to speak someday, as he had been.

Though I'd had no interest in it before, I ran for a student council office, again at his suggestion.

I remember the summer before my senior year praying that I could start on the basketball team. I was sixth man at the time, and I wanted to start because I knew it would make Dad proud.

Did I mention I was the compliant kid in the family?

□ □ □   ▩

My relationship with my mom was different. She, like my dad, was a good person, decent and kind, but she wasn't outgoing, and rather than tell me stories from her childhood, she was full of make-believe stories. Though I never understood why, she was painfully shy in social settings, like church, or functions a coach's wife was expected to be at the center of. She seemed to carry a lot of shame inside.

I didn't understand the source of her shame until one night after my dad's funeral.

She had gone to bed, and her siblings were sharing stories around our table. One mentioned how hard my mother's childhood had been, how she'd suffered so much more than the other kids. She was in her most tender, impressionable years when her dad started drinking and gambling. He had borrowed so much money that the family feared loan sharks would either take the house or kill him, maybe both. All the kids went to work and gave their paychecks to cover the debts. Somehow they survived, and life stabilized. Without knowing all the details, I know that the home my mother grew up in, at least for a time, was full of such frightening turmoil that I can't begin to imagine how it impacted her.

If that wasn't enough shame to bear, my mother was left-handed, and attended a parochial school where left-handedness was believed to be from the devil. To train her to write with her right hand, her teacher tied her left hand behind her back. Can you imagine the taunts from her peers? Kids on the playground can be vicious.

My dad was also an outsider, in a way, but through sheer determination and an indomitable spirit he fought his way out of that neighborhood. My mother was a wonderful woman in so many ways, yet because of the shame of her childhood, she did not get through her formative years nearly as well. She was a highly sensitive person. She was artistic, and also good with words. Now that I think of it, we never went to Dad to ask how something was spelled; we always went to Mom.

Mom died this past year, after being a widow for a quarter of a century.

She and Dad gave me life. They loved me, cared for me, provided for me, protected me, taught me a lot along the way, and launched me into a better life than either of them had. For all those things I will always be grateful.

I will forever be their son, sharing their genes, their stories, something of who they were, something of their wholeness as well as their brokenness. Just as my children will forever share a part of me.

FOR DISCUSSION AND STUDY

1. Read the opening quote from Brené Brown. What parts of your life haven't fit with who you've thought you're supposed to be? What parts haven't fit with who others have said or implied you need to be? In what ways have you hustled to achieve and prove your worthiness?

2. Brown defines shame, which "corrodes the very part of us that believes we are capable of change," as the "intensely painful feeling or experience of believing that we are flawed and therefore unworthy of love and belonging." Is there anything about which you feel that if everyone knew the truth they would see you for the fraud you are, and wouldn't want to be around you?

3. When you were a kid or an adolescent, or even later, what did others say to you or about you that truly hurt?

4. When you ponder the lengths to which God will go to rescue you, and when you realize that nothing can stop him from pursuing you because he loves you, what or how do you feel? Can your soul feel its worth? If not, what is keeping you from experiencing his love?

GOD'S PASSION FOR THE OUTSIDER | 5

Those who recall Francis Thompson's haunting image of God as the Hound of Heaven, pursuing us down the halls of time, might well ask who, in fact, is the hound and who the quarry, whether we seek God or whether we are sought. If we try to answer the question on those terms, however, we stray into theological foolishness. What we discover, instead, is that all the while we have been pursuing God he has been rushing toward us with reckless love, arms flung wide to hug us home. God aches for every person, for every creature, indeed, for every scrap of life in all creation to be joined again in the unity that was its first destiny. So while we are crying out, "Where are you, God?" the divine voice echoes through our hiding places, "Where are you?" Indeed, the story of the Garden of Eden reminds us that it is God who calls out first, and to this we answer. God's yearning for us stirs up our longing in response. God's initiating presence may be ever so subtle—an inward tug of desire, a more-than-coincidence meeting of words and events, a glimpse of the beyond in a storm or in a flower—but it is enough to make the heart skip a beat and to make us want to know more.

—Howard Macy
Rhythms of the Inner Life

Who is the outsider?

It depends. Remember in school, learning how to use a compass? With the pencil it held, you put a point on your paper. Then you set the compass's angle, determining your radius. Then you put the sharp metal extension on what was to be the center, and you drew a circumference around that point. After drawing all the way around, you have a circle.

What caused difficulty, historically, was that the compass changed hands, and when it did, the center changed. The church, for example, believed the earth was the center of our solar system, and that the planets and the sun revolved around it. If you believed the same, you were an insider; if you didn't, you were an outsider. To be outside the church during its era of supreme power involved a number of things, none of which was good. You were shunned. Nobody could do business with you or socialize with you. You could be banished, never again to see your homeland or loved ones. You could be holed up in a castle keep or tortured in some ecclesiastical dungeon. You could be killed. And they never "just killed" anyone back then—they looked for cruel and unusual ways to do it, so as to deter others.

Biblically speaking, Frank Spina, in his thorough and impeccably researched book *The Faith of the Outsider*, shares a working definition.

> An "outsider" is any person or group that has not been especially chosen by God to be the vehicle of the world's restoration and reconciliation. Remarkably, there are several narratives where outsiders are not only explicitly presented as such, but where they are in a variety of ways actually shown to be superior to God's elect, the insiders. Sometimes these outsiders show more faith in, a greater sensitivity to, or a greater understanding of Israel's

deity; on other occasions they do something that promotes the agenda of Israel's God, their outsider status notwithstanding. There are even times when outsiders become insiders, so much so that they become indistinguishable from the chosen people Israel. Given the Bible's pronounced emphasis on Israel's exclusivity as a function of God's sovereignty and grace, such outsider stories warrant the closest scrutiny if for no other reason than that they have great value in providing context, nuance, and texture for the important election theme. More importantly, these stories actually magnify the emphasis on God's sovereignty and grace.

Non-biblically, whether you are an insider or an outsider depends on who does the circumscribing. It depends on the location of the center, and the radius determines the area within the circumference. The center, in my opinion, should be the love of God, which is his essence, the starting point in defining who he is.

The ultimate circumference is where *he* draws it. Who can be inside it? If we go by John 3:16, that would be "the world"— that is, everyone. And yet it seems that many of us are—to use Gregory Boyd's words in *Repenting of Religion: Turning from Judgment to the Love of God*—"obsessed with the perimeter." We feel it is our obligation to be gatekeepers regarding who comes through the doors of our church. Jesus, in the parable of the wheat and the tares, doesn't sound so preoccupied. Let them grow up together, he said; the God of the Harvest, in his own time, will do the separating (see Matthew 13:30).

I particularly like Edwin Markham's poem "Outwitted" in terms of how we should view the outsider who might differ from us in one way or another.

> He drew a circle that shut me out—
> Heretic, rebel, a thing to flout.

But love and I had the wit to win:
We drew a circle and took him in!

Life outside the community has always been a place of isolation and estrangement. In the animal world, for instance, a horse may put its headstrong offspring outside the herd, teaching it—and, by example, the other young horses—a lesson. A horse outside the herd is vulnerable. It has its legs to run with and its hooves to kick with, but that is all. It has no chance if a pack of wolves chases it down.

Inside the herd: safety in numbers. Outside: You're on your own.

□ □ □ ■

The first insiders, Adam and Eve, were also the first outsiders.

> When the woman saw that the tree was good for food, and that it was a delight to the eyes, and that the tree was desirable to make one wise, she took from its fruit and ate; and she gave also to her husband with her, and he ate. Then the eyes of both of them were opened, and they knew that they were naked; and they sewed fig leaves together and made themselves loin coverings.
>
> They heard the sound of the Lord God walking in the garden in the cool of the day, and the man and his wife hid themselves from the presence of the Lord God among the trees of the garden. Then the Lord God called to the man, and said to him, "Where are you?"
>
> Genesis 3:6–9 NASB

In shame, Adam and Eve covered themselves with fig leaves to hide from each other. In shame, they hid in the bushes from God. And we have been hiding ever since. The history of humankind, in fact, is a story of hiding, both individually and collectively. The history of God, on the other hand, is a story of searching— walking through gardens in the cool of the day . . . standing at wells in the heat of the day . . . traversing the road to Emmaus . . . calling down over the road to Damascus. . . .

The story of God is a chronicle of pursuit. An ongoing search for those in hiding—for those of us who, for whatever reason, are on the outside.

The divorced. The disabled. The unemployed. The bankrupt. The suddenly single mom. The chronically depressed dad. The elderly person who can no longer drive. Those who feel outside their families and their reunions. The one whose sexual identity is different from the majority. Those who feel outside their religion and its rituals. Those outside physical health or mental health. Outside of faith, hope, love. Outside of friendship. Outside of joy.

Maybe something they did put them on the outside. Maybe some shameful secret put them there. Maybe they got there simply by getting older, weaker, less useful. Or maybe the social insiders at middle school placed them there. Maybe their hair was too frizzy, their frame too gawky. Maybe their nose was too big or their breasts too small. Maybe stuttering made them the object of ridicule. Maybe they were unusually quiet, or constantly talkative.

If you, for whatever reason, feel like an outsider and are covering your true self or the truth of your story out of shame, I hope these words from Gregory Boyd's *Repenting of Religion* will cover you in a different way:

> As with Adam and Eve, whom God tenderly clothed to conceal their nakedness, we too are called to proclaim that God's love

"covers a multitude of sins" (1 Peter 4:8). God tenderly clothes us in our nakedness, our vulnerability to judgment, and our shameful depravity.

I love that God doesn't ridicule Adam and Eve for their flimsy attempts to cover themselves. I love that he isn't sarcastic. I love that he doesn't rip off their fig leaves and expose them in a sudden strip search.

Why?

Because love doesn't do things like that. *Love doesn't expose; it covers.*

The Pharisees, on the other hand, excelled at exposing other people's shame. Take the incident of the woman caught in adultery: in the act, the text says. Can you imagine, being torn from an embrace, naked, by a bunch of angry men and dragged through the streets, kicking and screaming?

Jesus refuses to be a part of this public humiliation. He covers her from the leering crowd, taking the attention off of her and directing it at the self-righteous vigilantes. He stands up to her accusers and stays with her until they skulk away. Cloaked in his kindness, she is given another covering before she leaves—his forgiveness.

Boyd continues:

In his mercy, the all-holy God works with us. When we fail in his plan A, he tenderly works with us on a plan B, and then a plan C, and then a plan D. For most of us, he's gone through the entire alphabet many times! "The steadfast love of the Lord never ceases, his mercies never come to an end" (Lamentations 3:22).

This is what God did with Adam and Eve. Eden was Plan A. When they failed, he didn't leave them to themselves, didn't abandon them, didn't start over with someone else. He came to them, called to them, clothed them. In his mercy, he expelled them from the garden, for if they had stayed they would have access to the Tree of Life, able to live longer but with a life that was in a continual state of decay.

East of Eden was Plan B. When the gates clanged shut behind them, Adam and Eve were no longer insiders; after that, no one was. Now everyone was born on the outside. God's plan would be to find these outsiders and, one by one, bring them back in.

He was just as passionate about this plan as he'd been about the original one. His design to save outsiders was encapsulated in the seed of a promise recorded in Genesis 3:15. One day, a descendant of our first parents would be born, a deliverer who would seek and save those who were lost; he would bring them in—bring them home—and in the process, eventually, he would destroy the enemies of God, from the devil to death itself.

But Cain killed Abel, the carrier of this seed; God went ahead to another plan. Again, he was as fully invested in this plan as he was in the other two. Metaphorically, he continued going down the alphabet.

Consider the woman at the well. She was an outsider by race, for the Jews had no dealings with the Samaritans. She was an outsider by gender, for women had few rights in that culture—they couldn't own property, couldn't worship with men, and had little or no voice in community affairs. She was an outsider because even within the Samaritans' mixed race and mixed religion, social mores were observed. She had been married five times, which would have put her at Plan E, except the last marriage didn't work out either, and this time she had decided to simply live with the man. And maybe by now she had given up on a plan—given up her dreams, relinquished her hope, ceased to believe she had any value. Let go of the thought that there just might be a man out there who understood and loved her for who she was.

How did the women of the city treat her? Her coming to the well at the day's hottest hour speaks volumes. The other women would have come early or late in the day when the sun was low on the horizon, when the air was cool. But this woman would rather bear the scorn of the sun than the searing stares of the supposedly more righteous.

How does Jesus treat this woman who was stumbling her way through the moral alphabet? He engages her in conversation, taboo for someone in his position. He talks with her kindly, respectfully. And then he speaks to her heart: "Go and get your husband."

She hides among the leaves of an evasive answer: "I don't have one."

He affirms that what she has said is true—that while she has had five husbands, she isn't married to the man she is living with now.

Why does he do this? To shame her? If so, to what end? There is no audience to curry favor with, and certainly he knows she has carried enough shame over the course of five failed marriages. No, he says this to let her know he understands her. He knows where she has been, what she's been looking for, even though love had proved as evasive and ephemeral as a desert mirage. She has gone from one dry well to another . . . and another . . . and another. She is tired, and thirsty.

This woman, with a life so full of failure, had given up on a plan. Then Jesus shares a plan that had been in the making since the foundation of the world. When she said she knew that Messiah was going to come someday, he stopped her and said: "I who speak to you am He" (see John 4:26 NASB).

Do you get the full weight of those words?

It is as if Jesus were saying to her: "The promise made to Adam and Eve is standing before your very eyes. The coming one has come, and you are talking with him. You have an audience with the King, and you have his undivided attention."

Jesus gives this unnamed outsider with a checkered past the clearest revelation of his identity in the Gospels. He doesn't do that with Pharisees when they question him, or with the High Priest, or with Pilate—he was vague with them, even evasive. But with her he reveals something prophets and angels standing on tiptoes with craned necks and cupped ears have been hoping to hear for two thousand years.

Howard Macy was right: "God aches for every person, for every creature, indeed, for every scrap of life in all creation to be joined again in the unity that was its first destiny."

She was just a scrap of life, outside the covenant community, outside her own community, scorched by the sun and by the scorn of her own people. But for this one life, this unrelenting Shepherd trekked across Samaritan desert to find.

That is how passionate he is about outsiders— about finding them, and bringing them home.

□ □ □ ■

Probably fifteen years ago, my brother flew out to visit me in Colorado. He didn't come for the scenery, to hike or to fish, or for business. He came for me. He came with a book, *Driven to Distraction*, written by two physicians, both of whom had attention deficit disorder. He had read the book, dog-eared some of its pages, and underlined certain parts.

"I think you have ADD," he said seriously. He showed me some of the symptoms ADD causes people to exhibit. Page after page I saw my life in print, the diagnosis slowly unfolding before me, with research substantiated by doctors.

This disorder is genetic and can now be discovered not only through testing but also through brain scans. He had me think through our family line to trace which members of our family likely had it. All were highly creative, and highly unfocused. ADD often comes in the package with an artistic temperament. So does ADHD, the type that manifests in physical hyperactivity, though mine was more mental than physical.

Not exactly exhilarating news, but oddly liberating.

One self-help book for people with ADD is *You Mean I'm Not Lazy, Stupid, or Crazy?* It's a good title, because that's how it feels if there's no clinical name for it. You can't get your work done with the ease or dependability others seem to demonstrate. You're not sure why, and the adjectives that come to mind usually are the ones in that book title. The result is that you start believing a lie about yourself. If you believe the lie long enough, it becomes the truth—at least, the truth as you perceive it.

□ □ □ ■

The weight of shame is cumulative. Year after year a little more collects. Though you box it away, over time you have boxes upon boxes, and pretty soon your mind has become a Sam's Club of Shame. If you have a child with ADD or ADHD, the biggest problem isn't her forgetfulness, or his trouble keeping his room clean, but the ongoing damage to your child's sense of worth.

The shame of perceiving self not merely as different but as deficient can make your child feel more and more of an outsider. "Alone on the outside" is a dangerous place for a kid. Especially if shame is what put him there, or her there.

Reading through the book my brother gave me, I felt encouraged. It gave a name to something I knew was different about me but hadn't identified. There was treatment for it; there were ways to manage it. (If you want to know what it's like unmanaged, read the first couple pages of Judith Guest's *Ordinary People*, where Conrad is lying on his bed, his thoughts bouncing all over the place like pinballs.)

On a bad day, the ADD brain is like having a roomful of preschoolers in your head, all out of their seats, climbing over desks, poking at each other, some whining at the window to go outside, others racing up and down the aisles, still others throwing erasers across the room at the ones by the window, while the teacher stands behind her desk, shouting at them to sit down and turn to page ten in their books.

I am exaggerating a tad, because it's not always that way. But sometimes I'll be trying to listen to someone, and some thought in my head, without provocation, will just get up and leave the room. I'm looking intently at the person talking with me, but I haven't heard the last five sentences. I try to concentrate so he doesn't think he is boring, for, as a highly sensitive person, I would feel terrible if he thought I thought that. My thought didn't "leave" because it was bored—it had all this nervous energy it needed to walk off.

Here's a good day with ADD: Those same "children," with help, can be compelled to sit still. And they can be amazing little helpers themselves—they come up with creative ideas, new ways of seeing, and original means of self-expression. Or maybe there's a book you need, or a quote, but you only vaguely remember where you last saw it. On a good day, an eager little helper knows just where to find it and retrieve it for you.

On a bad day you feel you have to offer the little ferrets Kool-Aid with an added pinch of something to calm them down, which is why a fair number of people with ADD struggle with drug and alcohol issues. A drink does calm down the classroom. After a second one, everyone's in their seats and you feel the way you imagine normal people feel. And that feels good because suddenly you don't feel so much like an outsider.

You do forget things and lose things, with ADD. And paper is pretty much your nemesis. How that plays itself out for a writer is that you start building little tenement slums of Xerox copies you're sure you're going to need for the current project, along with Post-It Notes inscribed with really, really important stuff. And there are books, articles, ideas you've jotted on 3x5's or napkins.

Another thing I learned from a therapist whose husband is a doctor with ADD: Structure is key because your mind, which sometimes can do truly wonderful things, can walk off the job. The ADD brain needs a certain amount of stimulation to get its thoughts out of bed and off to work. But if the brain gets overstimulated, it starts feeling overwhelmed and calls over its shoulder while leaving the building, "The heck with this. I'm outta here."

So you get behinder and behinder, more stressed, more overwhelmed. And . . .

And, well, then it's not funny anymore. You get frustrated and discouraged and down on yourself and—ever seen the movie

Network?—you feel you need a Howard Beal moment but you can't get the window open, and when you try to pick up the TV to throw it through the glass, you throw out your back instead, and then you think about jumping through the window yourself but it comes to you that you live in a one-story house.

"Okay, everyone back in your seats!"

I have to look at this with a sense of humor, because, quite honestly, it drives me crazy. Drives people around me a little crazy too. It fills me with shame and makes me feel like an outsider. I say terrible things to myself when I'm out there, alone and ashamed.

□ □ □ ▪

Fast forward a decade. My kids are grown and off to college and careers, to homes of their own and families of their own. That good life I felt would last forever, didn't. It slowly came unraveled. The more it did, the worse I got, the more alone I felt, the more ashamed, more abandoned, more angry.

Then, one day, the anger I had suppressed since childhood started spraying out as if sourced by a geyser. I thought and said and did things that shocked me. I had never in my adult life yelled—had felt almost incapable of doing so. I had never flipped off people on the highway, and suddenly I was doing that. I was seething with rage.

I finally went somewhere that treated people with anger traceable back to childhood trauma. For a week I listened to lectures, read, had group therapy, did art therapy, saw the way such trauma had affected the other men there.

Each of us, without exception, carried a deep sense of shame. Without exception, we felt we weren't good enough, worthy enough. At some time or another, in adulthood, we each had started living as if that lie were the truth.

I learned a lot about addictions, how they often were adult manifestations of pain rooted in childhood that never healed. It was never healed because it remained hidden. Shame is one of the elements that kept it hidden, locked away so no one would know.

Regrettably, the anger and unforgivenness weren't tidily packaged up and put behind me by the end of the week. When I arrived home, they actually got worse. I found myself grasping anger and unforgivenness with a clenched fist. It was willful, I knew that. I wanted my day in court to explain myself, defend myself. I wanted to tell someone off but wasn't sure who. I wanted to go fifteen rounds in the ring and slug it out with . . . *anyone*; it didn't matter.

C. S. Lewis once said he thought unforgivenness might be worse than murder. *Worse than murder?* I was skeptical when I first read it. But I finished reading, and it made perfect sense. Whereas murder may take place in a moment of passion, he argued, unforgivenness is a cold, deliberate decision we make every day. That was certainly true for me.

Jesus said as much in Matthew 5. It's a small step, for example, from throwing hateful words to throwing punches and landing one that might prove lethal.

I felt on the outside of everything.

Outside of even caring I was there.

FOR DISCUSSION AND STUDY

1. Not only do we often imagine that we are the ones pursuing God, but we also feel that he is nowhere to be found. Howard Macy advises us to remember that no matter what we perceive, God is passionately seeking us. Spend some time in prayer, thanking God for his love and his faithfulness. Ask him to vitalize and strengthen your ability to notice his nudges and follow his direction.

2. What do you feel outside of? That is, what do you believe eludes you what do you think you cannot find, cannot have, cannot enjoy? What is beyond your hope?

3. God is love. And love doesn't expose; it covers. So why do we flee from God? Why do we try everything we can think of to avoid being found? Is there a part of you that you don't want God to pursue, to "discover"?

4. When you're "out there, alone," what do you feel? What are the things you tell yourself?

GOD'S PROVISION FOR THE OUTSIDER | 6

Hospitality . . . means primarily the creation of a free space where the stranger can enter and become a friend instead of an enemy. Hospitality is not to change people, but to offer them space where change can take place.

—Henri J. M. Nouwen
Reaching Out

I t all goes back to Abraham.

When Abraham was brought into a covenantal relationship with God in Genesis 12, he was called to leave his country, where he was an insider, so to speak, to become an outsider in a foreign land.

The writer to the Hebrews underscores this.

> By an act of faith, Abraham said yes to God's call to travel to an unknown place that would become his home. When he left he had no idea where he was going. By an act of faith he lived in the country promised him, *lived as a stranger* camping in tents.
>
> 11:8–9, emphasis added

As a stranger traveling in a foreign land, Abraham depended on the kindness of those he encountered along the way. He in turn extended that same kindness to strangers he encountered. Genesis 18, for instance, tells of Abraham hosting three divine strangers, actually running to greet them, offering them his hospitality by giving them a safe place to rest and a savory meal to refresh themselves.

There is a large amount of Old Testament legislation to make sure Israel provided for outsiders, relating to everything from justice to rest to protection to provisions. Here's an example of one of those laws.

> When you are harvesting in your field and you overlook a sheaf, do not go back to get it. Leave it for the foreigner, the fatherless and the widow, so that the Lord your God may bless you in all the work of your hands. When you beat the olives from your trees, do not go over the branches a second time. Leave what remains for the foreigner, the fatherless and the widow. When you harvest the grapes in your vineyard, do not go over the vines again. Leave what remains for the foreigner, the fatherless and the widow. Remember that you were slaves in Egypt. That is why I command you to do this.
>
> Deuteronomy 24:19–22 NIV

No legal provision, however, was more central or more sacred than hospitality, a pinnacle virtue in the ancient Near East. The relationship between host and guest was sacred; hospitality was the process of inviting outsiders inside, which changed them from strangers to guests. This differed from simply entertaining family and friends within your social circle. In Genesis 18 and 19, we see Abraham, then Lot showing hospitality to visiting strangers. The writer to the Hebrews uses these two incidents to show that heaven's purposes are often accomplished through us: "Do not forget to show hospitality to strangers, for by so doing some people have shown hospitality to angels without knowing it" (13:2 NIV).

The concept of hospitality shown to those who are far from home is expressed by *philoxenia,* a word used in both classical and biblical Greek. As *philo* means "friend" and *xenia* (from which we get "xenophobia") means "stranger," the compound means "friend of the stranger." *Philo* also is a Greek word for "love" and so *philoxenia* can be translated "love of the stranger."

It's interesting to note that there are far more Old Testament commands to love the stranger than to love your neighbor. Leviticus 19:34 is one: "The stranger who resides with you shall be to you as the native among you, and you shall love him as yourself, for you were aliens in the land of Egypt; I am the Lord your God" (NASB).

Hospitality is a way in which we show love to others. And love shown a stranger closely reflects God's divine love (see Luke 14:12–14; 6:32–35).

The best material I have read on hospitality comes from Henri Nouwen's *Reaching Out: The Three Movements of the Spiritual Life.* I seldom say this about a book, but his section on hospitality can change your life. If you're a teacher or a pastor, it may change not only how you think about your work, but how you go about it.

> While visiting the University of Notre Dame, where I had been a teacher for a few years, I met an older experienced professor who had spent most of his life there. And while we strolled over the beautiful campus, he said with a certain melancholy in his voice, "You know . . . my whole life I had been complaining that

my work was constantly interrupted, until I discovered that my interruptions were my work."

When I first read this, I had to close the book and take a walk to think. I thought about Jesus, how much he was interrupted, and how many incredible events took place because he stopped and took time for the interrupter.

If you're a parent, Nouwen's perspective on hospitality might change not only the way you see your children but how you treat them:

> This may sound strange, to speak of the relationship between parents and children in terms of hospitality. But it belongs to the center of the Christian message that children are not properties to own and rule over, but gifts to cherish and care for. Our children are our most important guests, who enter into our home, ask for careful attention, stay for a while and then leave to follow their own way.

Creating a space and inviting the stranger in creates an opportunity for transformative happenings; beautiful friendships can be forged, wondrous gifts can be shared, and strangers can be turned into friends. First, though, we must be willing to be interrupted, even inconvenienced. We must learn to live from a place of faith rather than fear. And we must become a good host—which, perhaps, isn't the same as what we imagine a good host to be.

> Hosts often feel that they have to talk all the time to their guests and entertain them with things to do, places to see, and people to visit. But by filling up every empty corner and occupying every empty time their hospitality becomes more oppressive than revealing.

Being a good host is realizing that hospitality is about fashioning, not filling, a space. When a hospitable space is produced, amazing things happen. The host *not* cramming it full from wall to wall leaves room for the Holy Spirit to flutter around in it, hovering as he did over the primordial deep and infusing it with life.

□ □ □   ■

If we are to love the stranger who resides *with* us, and hospitality is a way of expressing that love, then it follows that we should show hospitality to the stranger.

Which raises a question.

What about the stranger who resides *in* us? The part of us that is an alien in a foreign land. The part of us that is an outsider. How do we treat *that* stranger?

Taking a cue from Leviticus 19:34—"The stranger who resides with you shall be to you as the native among you, and you shall love him as yourself"—gives one pause.

We can ignore that part of us. We can deny it lives in us. We can hide it from others, even from ourselves. We can try to send the alien back to where it came from.

Or, we can be a good host and create a space where we can learn to converse, listen, understand. Shame, for example—what *do* you do with it? Here's a thought. Welcome it. Treat it like a guest. Have it sit down in your living room. Listen to its story.

Hello, Shame. I know you're in there, in me, hiding in the closet. How about coming out so we can talk? Here, sit on the couch. Let me get you something to eat, and then I want to hear your story. Not too fast, I have lots of time. I would really like to know where you've been, how you got here, and what happened to you along the way. Everything.

Anger! Hey, let's take a break and sit on the porch swing. Help me understand all that grinding of the teeth, that muttering and shouting in the car. Tell me about you. You seem hurt. Why don't you do the talking, and I'll just listen? I really want to understand.

And unforgivenness. Can we talk?

□ □ □ ■

If we are to love the stranger as we love ourselves, and if we are to show hospitality to that stranger as if he were native to our land, then we have to at least start communicating. Then maybe we can create a space where change can take place, where the Holy Spirit can do what he does best.

Now back to Abraham, where this all started. In *Anatheism,* Richard Kearney writes:

> The great founder of biblical religion is capable of both hostility and hospitality. And Abraham's descendants have followed suit throughout history. Reject the stranger or embrace the stranger. In fact, the annual Jewish festival of Sukkot serves to remind the followers of Abraham that they are forever tent dwellers, strangers on the earth committed to the hosting of strangers. This is a reminder that needs to be made again and again, year after year. Why? Because biblical religion, like most other religions, is capable of the best and of the worst. It all comes down, in the first and last instance, to a wager of faith—a hermeneutic reading of the word of God. . . . Abraham's heartless banishment of Hagar and Ishmael is totally at odds with his hospitable reaction to the arrival of the aliens from nowhere. Capable of the most cruel acts, Abraham is capable of receiving potentially threatening nomads into his home with open arms. As a result of his radical turning around, he opens himself and his wife Sarah to new life.

Open yourself to new life. Choose faith over fear, hospitality over hostility. Are there risks? Kearney answers:

> The stranger, in short, is the uninvited one with nowhere to lay his head unless we act as "hosts" and provide a dwelling. There is a sense of surprising interruption about the coming of this estranged and estranging outsider—a sense of unknowability calling for risk and adventure on our part.

There *are* risks to inviting in the stranger.

But are they really greater than the risks of sending him away?

For, as Jesus asid, "I was a stranger, and you did not invite Me in." And the consequence of that refusal proved eternal.

FOR DISCUSSION AND STUDY

1. Reread Henri Nouwen's thoughts about hospitality and how hosts often feel they need to fill the space with talk and entertainment. What are the first things you think of when you hear the word *hospitality*? Who have been your most memorable or reliable examples of creating an environment of hospitality?

2. An older professor told Nouwen that his whole life had been one of complaint that his work was constantly interrupted, until he discovered that interruptions *were* his work. What did he mean by that? How might it look, practically, for you to apply such an outlook to your life?

3. In what ways did your parents approach raising you as a gift to cherish rather than a property to own and rule? In what ways was this not the case? How have you approached raising your children? How could you improve upon your view of child rearing?

4. Read Leviticus 19:34. What part of *you* is an outsider, an "alien"? Whether shame, anger, or unforgiveness has separated you from others, how can you place faith over fear, choose risk over rigidity, and embrace hospitality toward—create a space for, enter into dialogue with, show love to—strangers?

JESUS' MISSION TO THE OUTSIDER | 7

The Spirit of the Lord is on me,
because he has anointed me
to proclaim good news to the poor.
He has sent me to proclaim freedom for the prisoners
and recovery of sight for the blind,
to set the oppressed free. . . .

—Luke 4:18 NIV

When I started researching the subject of outsiders in the Bible, I was startled to discover that Jesus, though he made himself available to everyone, didn't pursue everyone. But the passion of his life formed the pattern of his ministry. From his first breath to his last he constantly, relentlessly pursued the outsider.

☐ MISSION TO THE OUTSIDER: FORESHADOWED IN HIS GENEALOGY

The frontispiece of Matthew's gospel is a beautifully structured family tree.

In verse 1, he tells us that Messiah's lineage is traced through two of Israel's heroes: David, its greatest king, and Abraham, its greatest patriarch.

Then, in verse 17, he reveals that the genealogy is arranged as a literary triptych, something like those old room dividers with three hinged-together panels. Inscribed on each "panel" are fourteen generations. The first records the fourteen generations from Abraham to David; the second, from David to the Babylonian exile; the third, from the exile to Messiah.

It's all very measured. If we read it aloud we notice a distinct rhythm to the lines—until we get to the five phrases I've italicized (vv. 1-17 NIV), where interrupted rhythm causes a lyrical stumble. Tripping up the reader several times is the writer's way of not letting the fact slip by that *this* genealogy differs from others that had been included in the Old Testament. Something is about to happen that has been millennia in the making.

This is the genealogy of Jesus the Messiah the son of David, the son of Abraham:

Abraham was the father of Isaac,
Isaac the father of Jacob,
Jacob the father of Judah and his brothers,
Judah the father of Perez and Zerah, *whose mother was Tamar,*
Perez the father of Hezron,
Hezron the father of Ram,
Ram the father of Amminadab,
Amminadab the father of Nahshon,
Nahshon the father of Salmon,
Salmon the father of Boaz, *whose mother was Rahab,*
Boaz the father of Obed, *whose mother was Ruth,*

Obed the father of Jesse,
and Jesse the father of King David.

David was the father of Solomon, whose mother had been
Uriah's wife,
Solomon the father of Rehoboam,
Rehoboam the father of Abijah,
Abijah the father of Asa,
Asa the father of Jehoshaphat,
Jehoshaphat the father of Jehoram,
Jehoram the father of Uzziah,
Uzziah the father of Jotham,
Jotham the father of Ahaz,
Ahaz the father of Hezekiah,
Hezekiah the father of Manasseh,
Manasseh the father of Amon,
Amon the father of Josiah,
and Josiah the father of Jeconiah and his brothers at the time
of the exile to Babylon.

After the exile to Babylon:
Jeconiah was the father of Shealtiel,
Shealtiel the father of Zerubbabel,
Zerubbabel the father of Abihud,
Abihud the father of Eliakim,
Eliakim the father of Azor,
Azor the father of Zadok,
Zadok the father of Akim,
Akim the father of Elihud,
Elihud the father of Eleazar,
Eleazar the father of Matthan,
Matthan the father of Jacob,
and Jacob the father of Joseph, the husband of Mary, *and
Mary was the mother of Jesus* who is called the Messiah.

Thus there were fourteen generations in all from Abraham to David, fourteen from David to the exile to Babylon, and fourteen from the exile to the Messiah.

Isolating these particular lines indicates what the author is trying to do.

whose mother was Tamar
whose mother was Rahab
whose mother was Ruth
whose mother had been Uriah's wife
and Mary was the mother of Jesus

The inclusion of these five women in Messiah's genealogy would have immediately gotten the attention of the Jewish reader—Matthew's intended audience—for it was not customary for the Jews' records to include women. Even more remarkable is his inclusion of foreign women—intermarriage between Jews and foreigners was strictly prohibited—along with women whose morals were suspect if not altogether scandalous.

Tamar, for example, was a Canaanite, an outsider. You can read her story in Genesis 38:6–30.

Frank Spina, in *The Faith of the Outsider,* summarizes her impact, saying that without Tamar preserving the line of the promised seed, even though by deceit, there would have been no David.

It was Tamar, who as an outsider . . . acted in a manner that was decisive for the future of God's people and God's world. She was not originally an elected insider, but she saw to it that the chosen people's mission stayed on course. God used her to ensure that the insiders and their mission had a future.

Rahab was not only a Canaanite but also a harlot. You can read her story in Joshua 2:1–24 and 6:22–24.

She was an outsider to the covenant community, both racially and morally. Her people were despised. Her profession was despised. And yet, when she heard about the God of the Jews and how he had miraculously delivered them, her heart melted and she believed, giving her the courage to risk her life for his people. As a result, the writer to the Hebrews places her alongside some of the Old Testament's greatest heroes (11:30–31).

Rahab's inclusion into that place of honor tells us so much about God's love, which not only covers her but also celebrates her. She later married Salmon, who some believe was one of the spies she sheltered. In Ruth 4:21, we learn that her son was Boaz, who married the next woman in the Messiah's genealogy. As Spina comments:

> A woman who was an outsider of the lowly level of a Canaanite prostitute becomes an insider of the magnitude of a mother of the faith. She becomes the ancestress of both the great Israelite David (Ruth 4:18–22) and Jesus Christ.

Ruth was a foreigner from the land of Moab. You can read her story in the book of Ruth.

She was another outsider who, by the grace of God, became an insider. She was a woman of great character who won the heart of Boaz. He had chanced upon her as she was gleaning in his field, something only the poor and the sojourner were permitted to do, and he fell in love with her.

Here is the puzzling thing. Boaz took Ruth to the elders at the town's gate, where business was conducted, and asked them to bless the union. They wholeheartedly *did*, wishing the couple many children.

But the law forbade Jews from marrying foreigners.

How do we reconcile the elders' decision?

Boaz wasn't looking for a loophole; he was looking beyond the law of God to something greater—*the heart of God*. God's heart is for the outsider. His one grand mission—to find the lost one and bring her home—arches over every lesser mission between heaven and earth. Spina explains:

> It would be erroneous to think of God's electing Israel as a divine action calculated to benefit the chosen people to the exclusion of everyone else. While Israel's insider status as a result of its divine election is never in doubt, it has to be kept in proper theological perspective. God did not choose Israel in order to preserve Israelites while condemning all others. That is not the way either election or exclusion works in the Old Testament. Israel was not chosen to keep everyone else out of God's fold; Israel was chosen to make it possible for everyone else eventually to be included.

Bathsheba, an outsider, is not named but is implied in Matthew's saying that she'd been the wife of Uriah the Hittite, one of King David's mighty men and an outsider. You can read their story in 2 Samuel 11 and beyond.

David had an adulterous affair with Bathsheba, eventually leading to her husband's murder, and, after a cover-up, took her as his own wife. Though God took that baby, he gave them another one. The text says the Lord loved the baby, whom they named Solomon. And it was through the blessing of this once-scandalous union that the Savior of the world came.

☐ MISSION TO THE OUTSIDER: PICTURED AT HIS BIRTH

The setting of the Savior's birth and the people who came to celebrate it give us a depiction of his status and of his appeal.

There was no room for him in the inn; the only place for him was outside in a barn. The only ones to welcome his arrival—shepherds and astrologers—were themselves outsiders. Sheep herders, on the filthy fringe of society, were often transients and therefore suspect. The visitors from the East, foreigners involved in forbidden arts, were no less cause for suspicion.

Jesus, the ultimate insider, became an outsider in order to draw outsiders to himself and make them insiders.

☐ MISSION TO THE OUTSIDER: FORETOLD IN THE OLD TESTAMENT

When Jesus began his ministry, he announced it in his hometown.

> He came to Nazareth, where He had been brought up; and as was His custom, He entered the synagogue on the Sabbath, and stood up to read. And the book of the prophet Isaiah was handed to Him. And He opened the book and found the place where it was written,
>
> "THE SPIRIT OF THE LORD IS UPON ME, BECAUSE HE ANOINTED ME TO PREACH THE GOSPEL TO THE POOR. HE HAS SENT ME TO PROCLAIM RELEASE TO THE CAPTIVES, AND RECOVERY OF SIGHT TO THE BLIND, TO SET FREE THOSE WHO ARE OPPRESSED, TO PROCLAIM THE FAVORABLE YEAR OF THE LORD."
>
> And He closed the book, gave it back to the attendant and sat down; and the eyes of all in the synagogue were fixed on Him. And He began to say to them, "Today this Scripture has been fulfilled in your hearing."
>
> Luke 4:16–21 NASB

When Jesus arrived in Nazareth, which was little more than a hovel of outsiders, he identified himself as the divinely appointed

Servant prophesied by Isaiah. He came with the anointing of God to accomplish the mission of God: a search-and-rescue mission for outsiders. He had something for everyone on the outside, he said. For the poor—good news. For the prisoner—release. For the blind—recovery.

The message was greeted with ambivalence. Some welcomed his words; others resisted. Sensing the hostility building, Jesus addressed the issue of the hardheartedness of these insiders.

> He said to them, "No doubt you will quote this proverb to Me, 'Physician, heal yourself! Whatever we heard was done at Capernaum, do here in your hometown as well.'" And He said, "Truly I say to you, no prophet is welcome in his hometown. But I say to you in truth, there were many widows in Israel in the days of Elijah, when the sky was shut up for three years and six months, when a great famine came over all the land; and yet Elijah was sent to none of them, but only to Zarephath, in the land of Sidon, to a woman who was a widow. And there were many lepers in Israel in the time of Elisha the prophet; and none of them was cleansed, but only Naaman the Syrian." And all the people in the synagogue were filled with rage as they heard these things; and they got up and drove Him out of the city, and led Him to the brow of the hill on which their city had been built, in order to throw Him down the cliff. But passing through their midst, He went His way.
>
> vv. 23–30

Frank Spina says about this passage:

> Jesus appeals to two outsider stories in the Jewish Scriptures to make a point. He cites the fact that of all the widows in Israel during the time of Elijah, that great prophet was sent to a widow *outside* Israel to get help during a great famine (1 Kings 17:8–24). Jesus also calls attention to the fact that, of all the

lepers in Israel during the time of the prophet Elisha, the latter healed Naaman [the Syrian] alone (2 Kings 5).

Jesus aroused such enmity because he essentially was showing insiders that God, even in times past, had overlooked them in favor of those outside.

☐ **MISSION TO THE OUTSIDER: ILLUSTRATED BY THE DISCIPLES HE CHOSE**

The men Jesus chose to be his closest followers were not the best and the brightest. Most were from the region around the Sea of Galilee—*not* where a serious rabbi would look for students, but there Jesus gathered his. An odd lot by any standard—fishermen, a tax collector, a political activist, and a few others with unimpressive credentials.

☐ **MISSION TO THE OUTSIDER: EXPLAINED IN HIS TEACHING**

You need to know that I have other sheep in addition to those in this pen. I need to gather and bring them, too. They'll also recognize my voice. Then it will be one flock, one Shepherd.

John 10:14–16

"This pen" refers to Israel. "Other sheep" refers to those outside the covenant community or those Jews with some uncleanness— whether physical, mental, or moral—who had been butted from the fold by the other sheep. Jesus became an outsider—a stranger in his own land, who came to his own though his own did not receive him—to befriend outsiders. He was and still is the champion of all who have been pushed beyond the pen's perimeter—the poor, the oppressed, the rejected, the marginalized and disenfranchised, the forgotten and the forlorn, the shunned and the scorned.

☐ MISSION TO THE OUTSIDER: SEEN IN WHERE HE STARTED MINISTRY

After Jesus was baptized in the Jordan River, he didn't start his ministry in Jerusalem but in Galilee. Luke records his itinerary in chapter 4 of his gospel.

> Jesus returned to Galilee in the power of the Spirit, and news about Him spread through all the surrounding district. And He began teaching in their synagogues and was praised by all.
>
> vv. 14–15 NASB

For a century and a half before Jesus was born, the area around the Sea of Galilee was not populated primarily by Jews but by Gentiles—craftsmen, fishermen, farmers, and merchants who capitalized on the trade routes that ran through the area. Roman influence was more pronounced there than down south in Jerusalem. Rome brought in building projects, a welcomed boost to the local economy, and stationed large companies of soldiers there who needed food, supplies, and a variety of pleasures to sate their carnal appetites. The term *Galilean* was synonymous with *outsider.* They were half-breeds, a mongrel collection of mixed marriages, mingled accents, skin colors, and pagan influences. Jews had a presence in the area, with synagogues in cities of any size, but they were a minority, and most were not orthodox.

☐ MISSION TO THE OUTSIDER: SEEN IN THE AUDIENCE FOR HIS GREATEST SERMON

The audience Jesus addressed when he gave the Sermon on the Mount was not for the most part made up of insiders but outsiders. His words are recorded in Matthew 5–7. Verse 1 of chapter 5 prepares us before he begins: "When Jesus saw the crowds, He went up on the mountain; and after He sat down, His disciples came to Him" (NASB). The people in this crowd? They can be found at the end of Matthew 4:

> Jesus was going throughout all Galilee, teaching in their synagogues and proclaiming the gospel of the kingdom, and healing every kind of disease and every kind of sickness among the people. The news about Him spread throughout all Syria; and they brought to Him all who were ill, those suffering with various diseases and pains, demoniacs, epileptics, paralytics; and He healed them. Large crowds followed Him from Galilee and the Decapolis and Jerusalem and Judea and from beyond the Jordan.
>
> vv. 23–25 NASB

Syrians. Galileans. People from the ten Gentile cities, known as the Decapolis. Those from beyond the Jordan. *Outsiders.* The ones who came from Jerusalem and Judea were a fraction of the multitude.

Why did the crowds come? Because Jesus had healed them. All the ones who were outside of health, those judged to be unclean and unfit, the outcasts—they followed Jesus and gathered to hear him speak.

☐ MISSION TO THE OUTSIDER: DEMONSTRATED IN HIS EMBRACE OF SAMARITANS

The Samaritan race originated when Assyria took most of Israel's northern kingdom into captivity in the eighth century BC. The invaders repopulated the vacated area with foreigners, who then intermarried with some of the Jews the Assyrians had left behind. When the Jews who'd been taken captive eventually returned to their land, they considered these Samaritans half-breeds and shunned them. A racial and theological rift developed between the two groups and continued to widen, up to when Jesus entered the scene.

Because Jesus' mission was to outsiders, though, he had a different approach. He reached out to the Samaritans. Among just the few instances that were recorded, he healed a Samaritan leper; he refused to listen to his disciples when they wanted him to destroy a Samaritan village for rejecting him; he cast a Samaritan as hero in his illustration of being a good neighbor; and he flung open the gates of his kingdom by a woman who was an outsider to the outsiders who lived there.

☐ MISSION TO THE OUTSIDER: DRAMATIZED AT THE CLEANSING OF THE TEMPLE

During one Passover, in Jerusalem, we see something in Jesus that caught a lot of people, including his disciples, off guard. We see him angry. As Matthew records the incident:

> Jesus went straight to the Temple and threw out everyone who had set up shop, buying and selling. He kicked over the tables of loan sharks and the stalls of dove merchants. He quoted this text:
>
> *My house was designated a house of prayer;*
> *You have made it a hangout for thieves.*
>
> Now there was room for the blind and crippled to get in. They came to Jesus and he healed them.
>
> 21:12–14

It was not *what* the merchants were doing so much as *where* they were doing it. The text Jesus quoted, from Isaiah 56, explains:

As for the outsiders who now follow me,
    working for me, loving my name,
    and wanting to be my servants—
All who keep Sabbath and don't defile it,
    holding fast to my covenant—
I'll bring them to my holy mountain
    and give them joy in my house of prayer.
They'll be welcome to worship the same as the "insiders,"
    to bring burnt offerings and sacrifices to my altar.
Oh yes, my house of worship
    will be known as a house of prayer *for all people,*

vv. 6–7, emphasis added

The Court of the Gentiles, where the temple cleansing took place, was the architectural statement of faith that God would make good on his promise to Abraham. This court, built on the foundational belief that outsiders would come, was reserved especially for the outsider so there would be a quiet and hospitable place where he could pray.

The merchants and moneychangers profaned that sacred space with noise and clutter. Notice that once the space was cleared there was room for the blind and the crippled to come hobbling in. And when they did, what did Jesus do? He healed them.

That's why he did what he did—*for the outsiders who had been crowded out.*

☐ MISSION TO THE OUTSIDER: IMMORTALIZED IN HIS LAST PARABLE

For the Passion Week, Jesus came to Jerusalem one last time. The words he spoke were last words, both to the people and to his disciples; his acts were last acts—last gestures, last meals, one last healing, one last rescue. Last things are weighty things, sometimes capturing a lifetime of emotion or an eternity of truth.

This was his last parable:

When he finally arrives, blazing in beauty and all his angels with him, the Son of Man will take his place on his glorious throne. Then all the nations will be arranged before him and he will sort the people out, much as a shepherd sorts out sheep and goats, putting sheep to his right and goats to his left.

Then the King will say to those on his right, "Enter, you who are blessed by my Father! Take what's coming to you in this kingdom. It's been ready for you since the world's foundation. And here's why:

"I was hungry and you fed me,
I was thirsty and you gave me a drink,
I was homeless and you gave me a room,
I was shivering and you gave me clothes,
I was sick and you stopped to visit,
I was in prison and you came to me."

Then those "sheep" are going to say, "Master, what are you talking about? When did we ever see you hungry and feed you, thirsty and give you a drink? And when did we ever see you sick or in prison and come to you?" Then the King will say, "I'm telling the solemn truth: Whenever you did one of these things to someone overlooked or ignored, that was me—you did it to me."

Then he will turn to the "goats," the ones on his left, and say, "Get out, worthless goats! You're good for nothing but the fires of hell. And why? Because—

"I was hungry and you gave me no meal,
I was thirsty and you gave me no drink,
I was homeless and you gave me no bed,

I was shivering and you gave me no clothes,
Sick and in prison, and you never visited."

Then those "goats" are going to say, "Master, what are you talking about? When did we ever see you hungry or thirsty or homeless or shivering or sick or in prison and didn't help?"

He will answer them, "I'm telling the solemn truth: Whenever you failed to do one of these things to someone who was being overlooked or ignored, that was me—you failed to do it to me."

Then those "goats" will be herded to their eternal doom, but the "sheep" to their eternal reward.

Matthew 25:31–46

☐ MISSION TO THE OUTSIDER: UNDERSCORED BY HIS BELOVED DISCIPLE

Many have memorized the words of Jesus in John 3:16, but fewer have memorized what he said immediately after. John the disciple, "the one Jesus loved dearly" (John 13:23), recorded the conversation between Jesus and Nicodemus that included the following:

For God so loved the world, that he gave his only begotten Son, that whosoever believeth on him should not perish, but have eternal life. For God sent not the Son into the world to judge the world; but that the world should be saved through him. He that believeth on him is not judged: he that believeth not hath been judged already, because he hath not believed on the name of the only begotten Son of God.

John 3:16–18 ASV

This depiction of the human condition shows us all to be outsiders, meaning we are all already judged. Not the sort of portrait you want to hang in your office.

If a decorator were redoing your office in a nautical motif, with blues and grays and paintings of ships, which seafaring vessel might best fit with the biblical view of the post-Eden human condition?

The *Titanic*.

We all know it was thought to be unsinkable. But during its maiden voyage on the moonless night of April 14, 1912, that massive liner struck an iceberg in the frigid North Atlantic waters. The berg scraped the ship's hull, popping rivets and separating steel plates on its starboard side. The gash wasn't huge; rather, the pressure to which the iceberg had subjected the plates caused separations at the rivets. Most of these "gaps" were between just one-quarter and three-quarters of an inch in width. The total area open to the sea was only about twelve square feet.

Many sleeping passengers weren't even awakened by the collision. Others felt it but thought nothing of it. Virtually all went back to what they were doing.

However, the captain instructed wireless operators to start sending out distress signals. He also sent orders to the staff to wake the passengers and tell them to don life jackets and get into the lifeboats.

At first the passengers thought the crew was overreacting. After all, this was the safest ocean liner ever made. Everything *seemed* fine, so people were not alarmed. The first few lifeboats lowered were only half full; most didn't want to expose themselves to chilly weather and the bother of it all.

□ □ □ ■

The *Carpathia* was the one ship with a chance to get there; certainly it wouldn't come within the two hours the captain estimated until the *Titanic* would sink. Lifeboats were everyone's only hope . . . and, then, that the *Carpathia* would arrive to rescue them before they froze on the open sea.

The ultimate message from the crew to the passengers was: "The ship is sinking. You will go down with it if you don't get in the lifeboat."

Essentially, that is the message of John 3:16–18.

The mission of Jesus wasn't to send the ship to the bottom of the sea; that already was happening. He came to save those who were sinking.

The lifeboat *is* Jesus.

And our role is simple: to help as many as we can into the lifeboat.

The band played all night to the bitter, freezing end. It is rumored to have begun with "Ragtime" and ended with "Nearer My God to Thee."

The *Carpathia* arrived early that morning.

The only survivors were those in the lifeboats.

Just 745 were saved; 1,595 had perished.

☐ MISSION TO THE OUTSIDER: SEEN IN HIS LAST RESCUE

From the cross next to him, an outsider called to Jesus, asking to be remembered when he came into his kingdom. And shortly before he died, Jesus helped one more into the lifeboat.

FOR DISCUSSION AND STUDY

1. What specific occurrences or stations in life made the following people in the Bible outsiders?

   • Tamar

   • Rahab

   • Ruth

   • Bathsheba

   • Mary

   • The shepherds

   • The Magi

   What contemporary examples can you cite that would place someone in a position to be considered an outsider?

2. Regarding God's emphasis on his pursuit of outsiders, in what ways can you see the church of our time resembling "the insiders" in the time of Jesus? Read Matthew 20:1–16 (the parable of the workers). These men resented someone else being given grace, even though nothing had been withheld that was coming to them. If God had rescued you at a very young age, and then you'd followed and served him throughout your life, how would you feel about his welcoming and celebrating someone who had, for instance, lived his entire life cursing God and seeking his own happiness? Could you rejoice with God over the finding of this lost lamb—no matter who it was? Is there anyone with whom you wouldn't want to share heaven?

3. How would thinking of your calling as "helping as many as you can into the lifeboat" affect the way you relate to others? What effect would it have on how and where you spend your time or other

resources? Would it alter your view toward or your treatment of any specific person or people?

4. What are some ways you could see yourself reaching out to those who are sinking? How could you help them to safety?

GOD'S MANDATE TO THE INSIDER | 8

The bodies of those animals whose blood is brought into the holy place by the high priest as an offering for sin, are burned outside the camp. Therefore Jesus also, that He might sanctify the people through His own blood, suffered outside the gate. So, let us go out to Him outside the camp, bearing His reproach. For here we do not have a lasting city, but we are seeking the city which is to come.

—Hebrews 13:11–14 NASB

"Outside the gate" and "outside the camp" were synonymous in Jewish thinking. The former term dates back to Israel's post-Egypt wilderness wanderings, where there were strict regulations on what was and was not allowed inside the camp of the fledgling nation. Later, when the camp was replaced by the walled city, the term evolved to "outside the gate."

What was *outside* was what was unclean. Outsiders—lepers, for example—were barred from feasts and festivals, weddings and funerals, worship and rituals . . . anywhere "insiders" congregated.

The inside was not to be contaminated by exposure to the uncleanness on the outside. To get inside, one had to go through ritual cleansings that had to be approved by the priesthood. If you couldn't pass muster, then in the eyes of others your status wasn't much different from the garbage and refuse dumped outside the camp.

The background to the reference in Hebrews 13 is the ritual prescribed on the Day of Atonement, Judaism's highest and most holy day. After the sacrifice was made, the following procedure was observed:

> The bull and the goat for the sin offerings, whose blood was brought into the Most Holy Place to make atonement, must be taken *outside the camp*; their hides, flesh and intestines are to be burned up. The man who burns them must wash his clothes and bathe himself with water; afterward he may come into the camp.
>
> Leviticus 16: 27–28 NIV, emphasis added

One of the things that could only be done "outside the gate" of Jerusalem was Roman execution. Crucifixions could only take place outside the southeastern-corner walls on a hill over-looking the Valley of Hinnom—the city's garbage dump. Ever since child sacrifices had been made there during the reigns of Ahaz and Manasseh, this place had been cursed. Scattered fires burned continuously, stoked with bones from family meals, sweepings from stable floors, and any other unclean thing out for disposal. Bodies of executed criminals were sometimes dumped there, if they had no relatives or if the relatives were too ashamed to claim them.

The pit was foraged by dogs and picked over by vultures. What they left was swarmed by hordes of intrepid rats and then ravenous squirms of maggots. It was all flies, heat, and the ubiquitous stench of death. No one went there but the shunned and the scavenging poor and those whose job it was to keep the city clean. This was the Valley of Hinnom, commonly called *Gehenna*—this "Valley of Death" was an apt symbol for eternal estrangement from God.

Jesus, who experienced his own estrangement from God while overlooking that valley, arrived as an outsider, born outside in a stable. And he lived outside during his relentless pursuit of outsiders: though foxes had holes, though birds had nests, the Son of Man had nowhere to lay his head (see Matthew 8:20). While he remained accessible to the insiders of the day, frequently talking with them, on occasion dining with them, and sometimes debating them, he never joined them. And he died an outsider, between outsiders.

The writer to the Hebrews calls us to go to Jesus out there. He calls us to go outside the camp and to "bear his reproach." To share his shame, his suffering, his aloneness, his forsakenness. Why?

Because city life will betray us into thinking we have arrived, that a city of some kind or another is the end of the journey of faith. And, that if we get through its gates, we will be insiders. Surrounded by walls that will protect us. In neighborhoods that will reflect us, mirroring an identity that will flatter us, fulfill us, give us the lives we have always hoped to find.

However, that is not what those who have gone before us have been hoping to find.

Each one of these people of faith died not yet having in hand what was promised, but still believing. How did they do it? They saw it way off in the distance, waved their greeting, and accepted the fact that they were transients in this world. People who live this way make it plain that they are looking for their true home. If they were homesick for the old country, they could have gone back any time they wanted. But they were after a far better country than that—heaven country. You can see why God is so proud of them, and has a City waiting for them.

Hebrews 11:13–16

It has been said that the central human condition is homesickness, an embedded longing within us for our true home. After living like this for long enough, though, the adventure of being a pilgrim, stranger, or foreigner in the world wears thin. Especially if you have a family. You want to settle someplace with good schools and safe neighborhoods and property that appreciates. If you can't find the land promised to you, then, the temptation is to fold up your tent and settle for something else, anything that feels safe and secure with walls and gates and strict membership requirements to keep the outsiders outside the gate where they belong. It may not be Eden, but the grounds are well-manicured, the maintenance is covered by contract, and the neighbors are, well, the kind of people you want as neighbors. And, let's be honest, they have the kind of kids you want *your* kids playing with.

So what's wrong with that?

In a way, nothing.

In another way, everything.

□ □ □ ■

Finding the lost sheep and bringing it home—Jesus' mission—also is meant to be ours. "As the Father has sent me, I am sending you" (John 20:21 NIV).

But our mission is sometimes lost when we leave the outside's cold for the inside's warmth. We can forget where we came from, who we once were, what it felt like on the outside. We begin to enjoy the fellowship of insiders, the privileges of insiders, the safety of insiders, the esteem of insiders. And before we know it, we lose touch with those on the outside, lose God's plan for them, his prayers for them, his passion for them.

We want to be friends with successful people we can network with, who live in nice neighborhoods and have well-behaved kids. Yet Jesus was a friend of sinners; he didn't want to be on the inside. He wanted to be with those on the wrong side of the tracks, in tenement slums, those who were disconnected and disenfranchised. That is the neighborhood he *chose*.

The question is: *Do I?*

Do you?

I have had a tender spot in my heart for the less fortunate since I was a little boy. As an adult I tried to impart that to my children. But it wasn't a way of life for me. I was never on any kind of search-and-rescue mission, as Jesus was. It was more a drop-spare-coins-in-the-cup-while-leaving-the-store kind of thing. If someone needed help, I stopped and helped—seldom any real inconvenience. A half hour out of my way to take someone somewhere. A fast-food meal. A place to stay for the night. A bus ticket home. Car repairs. Pocket-change stuff.

Nothing wrong with that. But I'd never pursued anyone on the outside, let alone relentlessly.

The more I loved Jesus, the more I wanted to. Or at least, the more I wanted to try.

□ □ □ ▪

I saw a woman on the corner near the post office where I dropped my mail. She caught my attention mainly because of the sign she was holding, which I thought was creative, and because her clothes looked as if someone had doused them in bleach.

The light had turned red, and I saw her walking down the sidewalk by waiting cars. *Good location,* I thought. I rolled down my window and gave her some money before the light went green. Her eyes caught mine, only for a second, then turned downward as she mumbled appreciation.

I would come by on different days after thinking about her, imagining what her life was like before she ended up here. I dropped off spare change or sack lunches or something to drink, wondering all the while about her story. I felt prompted by God to help, though I had no real idea what to say or to do.

One day I stopped in the post office parking lot and invited her to lunch across the street—*close by,* I thought, which might keep her from feeling threatened. She agreed.

She was weathered by the sun and the wind, which made her look older than she was. That she was about my older daughter's age surprised me. She seemed to have a speech impediment, or maybe she couldn't open her mouth wide enough to enunciate well. I wasn't sure.

Little by little she told me her story—matter-of-factly, without emotion. She had been a college student, a science major who particularly liked Carl Sagan.

"He died a few years ago, didn't he?" I said.

She nodded.

"How old was he when he died, do you know?"

"Let's see, he was born on [such-and-such date] and died on [such-and-such date], so that would make him—"

She was doing the math in her head, and the answer she gave was not how old in years but how old in *days*.

"How did you do that?" I asked, amazed. Turned out this was nothing amazing to her—her mind just worked that way. I tested her on a couple other things, and she did the same thing, answering in terms of many thousands of days.

Over the months I found her to be, despite all appearances to the contrary, not only literate but literate on different levels and in different cultures. She could speak several languages. One day when I took her to the grocery store she was holding a copy of Frank McCourt's Pulitzer-Prize-winning *Angela's Ashes*—the Spanish edition. I'd taken two years of Spanish in junior high but hadn't learned enough for it to be of much use. "Read me something," I said, so she read the back-cover copy, as flawlessly and smoothly as if Spanish were her first language.

I learned by observation that she had obsessive-compulsive disorder. When I think of OCD, images come to mind of Bill Murray in *What About Bob?* or Jack Nicholson in *As Good As It Gets*—humorous characterizations of different types. I was to learn, though, there really is nothing humorous about it. Watching her go through life was painful. For instance, she used up to three *bottles* of bleach to clean off germs from her contact with other people on that corner. She even wore dishwashing gloves to insulate her from contact.

Though she shared an apartment with an older man at the time, they were getting evicted, and she needed someone to help her move. I had a truck then, and I volunteered.

As I helped, I was instructed to glove my hands and put everything in garbage bags. When moving furniture, I found splotches where bleach had spilled on the carpet. There was so much stuff, and she didn't want to throw any of it away—she went through agony, deciding what to keep and what to put in the trash. In the end she tossed almost nothing; we put it all in my truck and headed for a storage unit full of already accumulated black bags.

I became friends with both of them and truly enjoyed their company. I think they enjoyed mine. We'd go together for dinner sometimes, at a place where we could sit down inside and talk. I'd take the man to a nearby bar for football and beers, and little by little I learned what it's like for an African-American to grow up in the U.S. What a different experience from mine.

He had a lot of anger inside, which, after learning about his past, I could understand. He was my age, and out of work. He'd been drafted for the Vietnam War and served in the Navy but didn't see combat. The Navy used him in its boxing league, and he toured Europe while "duking it out," mostly with white boys, in fights that always drew crowds. One thing he taught me was how to protect myself if ever I thought someone bigger and stronger was going to start a fight. Though I doubt I'll ever need this info, I feel good that I have it.

The woman sometimes would ask me to drive her to her favorite grocery store, a couple miles away, and then have me stop to drop a sandwich or two at the back fence of a yard holding dogs she was fond of. Also, whenever she saw another woman on the street, she'd fill a plastic sack and hop out to give it to her. She wouldn't stay to talk; she'd just hand off the bag as she wished her luck.

I shared their story with my men's group, and they all passed the hat one morning. With what was collected, I was able to take the man to get his driver's license and then car insurance, with enough leftover money to buy clothes for a job interview.

We found a dentist willing to give them free dental work, and I looked at a number of programs that would take the woman, clean her up, and give her medical care, OCD treatment, job training, everything. I wanted to find someplace really, really clean because I knew that otherwise there was no chance she'd go through the front door.

I felt positive about what was happening, felt I was doing something meaningful, something that was on God's heart, and this made me feel good.

She resisted being admitted anywhere—calmly, but firmly. I tried to reason with her calmly and firmly. She listened. She nodded. And it seemed we were getting somewhere. But ultimately she was afraid. She had gone down that road before and was skeptical about revisiting it. Maybe she'd had bad drug reactions, or been abused when in treatment. I don't know.

"Please," I pleaded. "I will help you get help, but I cannot without your consent. I am not going to be here much longer. I don't want to see you die out there on that street, and that will happen someday if you don't get help."

She nodded. She knew. But, for whatever reason, she couldn't take that step. I had tried to build her trust in me, and she did trust me, but she didn't trust those on the inside of those buildings, those institutions, those men and women with their clipboards and white coats.

She was a voracious reader of books and magazines in several languages. If I asked if she needed a ride somewhere, she always wanted one, and most often to a bookstore or magazine stand. I remember one night being at a Barnes & Noble store until they were about to close. She put a few books on the counter to check out and then took wet, crumpled dollar bills, one by one, from her pocket. She had bleached each one after receiving it. The clerk didn't say anything to her but did pick up a microphone to summon some paper towels. When they arrived, he dried the bills individually before putting them in the till. I thought about how frustrating life must be for her and for those around her.

I took them to the theater a couple times; once we saw *The Wizard of Oz*. I thought the film might bring back some memories of their youth, some happy ones perhaps, and it did, I think. As the light flickered over their faces, I could see the kid in them, and this made me smile inside.

I wasn't prepared for the ending when it came, though I had seen the movie numerous times. Dorothy comes back to Kansas, waking with the words: "There's no place like home. . . . There's no place like home." And I realized then that they had no home to go back to. They had no home to look forward to either. They were outsiders, both, stranded on the sidewalk.

Eventually, though, I came to decide that I simply wasn't helping them. I felt it was ultimately a waste of time, money, energy. When I moved to another city, I didn't even say good-bye. I just left.

□ □ □ ■

During that time I saw a movie so compelling that immediately afterward I read the book.

The Soloist tells the true story of Steve Lopez's experience with Nathaniel Ayers, a talented musician and homeless schizophrenic living out of a grocery cart. Lopez had been trying to come up with a story for his *Los Angeles Times* column, and it struck him that Ayers might just be one.

He began investigating and learned Ayers had attended Juilliard for two years in the '70s before having to leave for "personal reasons" that all turned out to be associated with the sudden onset of schizophrenia. The book tells the story of their friendship as Lopez tries to get Ayers the help he needs to get off skid row and become a productive member of society. One of the journalist's impressions of the troubled musician:

> He plays for a while, we talk for a while, an experience that's like dropping in on a dream. Nathaniel takes nonsensical flights, doing figure-eights through unrelated topics. God, the Cleveland Browns, the mysteries of air travel and the glory of Beethoven. He keeps coming back to music. His life's purpose, it seems, is to arrange the notes that lie scattered in his head.

One particularly poignant moment in the film adaptation indicted me. When Lopez (Robert Downey Jr.) is frustrated that no attempt to help Ayers (Jamie Foxx) seems effective, a friend advises: "You can't fix LA, and you're never going to fix Nathaniel. Just be his friend and show up."

My failure was that I couldn't just be a friend and show up. I had wanted to get people off the street. To help the woman on the corner return to her sound mind. To bring her friend back to being the productive man he'd once been. Essentially, I was there to fix them. Maybe I needed to be needed, for whatever reason. Maybe I felt I needed to justify my existence somehow, validate my worth. Who knows? All I know is that I didn't help them.

In the final scene of *The Soloist*, in the music hall, the Los Angeles Philharmonic plays Beethoven, string quartets. The camera slowly pans across a row of the audience. First we see Nathaniel Ayers's sister, then Ayers, then Steve Lopez, and the visual holds as he "thinks through" his next column:

"Points West," by Steve Lopez (voiceover).

A year ago I met a man who was down on his luck and thought I might be able to help him. I don't know that I have helped him. Yes, my friend, Mr. Ayers, sleeps inside. He has a key, a bed. But his mental state and his well-being are as precarious now as the day we met.

There are people who tell me I've helped him, mental health experts who say that the simple act of being a friend can change brain chemistry, improve his functioning in the world. I can't speak for Mr. Ayers in that regard. Maybe our friendship has helped him, but maybe not.

I can, however, speak for myself. I can tell you that by witnessing Mr. Ayers' courage, his humility, his faith in the power of his art, I have learned the dignity of being loyal to something you believe in, holding on to it.

Above all else, I believe, without question, that it will carry you home.

In the end, I wasn't able to do for the woman or for the man what Mr. Lopez had done for Mr. Ayers. I tried to go to the outsider, because I believed it was the right thing to do and I believe God was prompting me to do it. *Was it for them?* I wonder now, looking back. *Was it for me?* I don't know. I felt I needed to get the woman off the street, into a facility that could treat her disorder, train her, find her a job, help her become self-sufficient. Bring her out of the cold into safety and warmth.

In the end, for all my education, all my training, all my experiences in life, I didn't know how to "just be a friend and show up."

In the end, she was still on the street.

And I was not carried home.

I was closer to God's heart—I could feel its familiar rhythm—but I was not home.

FOR DISCUSSION AND STUDY

1. When have you felt homesick? What have you reached toward for solace and security when you've felt you didn't belong or felt far from where you were comfortable?

2. Have you ever pursued someone "on the outside"? Have you ever pursued someone relentlessly? From your perspective, what has resulted from your pursuit?

3. Who do you know who hasn't tried to correct or fix but instead has been a friend and shown up? What have you learned through their demonstrations of friendship?

4. What opportunity or opportunities might you currently have to begin reaching out to someone in this way? How might you "go outside the camp" and "bear reproach," start sharing his shame, suffering, aloneness, or forsakenness?

THE PART OF ME THAT WAS FOUND | 9

Our sense of worthiness lives inside of our story. It's time to walk into our experiences and to start living and loving with our whole hearts.

—Brené Brown
The Hustle for Worthiness

Between writing the end of the last chapter and the beginning of this one, I moved another state away, another life away. Before I left, a lot of things happened that were sad and lonely and teetering-on-the-edge-of-the-cliff dangerous. I survived that time, this was the good news, but almost nothing else was good, or so it seemed to me.

Then something remarkable happened. Not at once, but a day at a time. Parts of me that had been lost felt as if they were being carried by someone bigger and stronger than me, someone who spoke in a so much kinder and gentler voice than I had been using on myself. Like shoots of life tufting through a long-encrusted snow covering, my feelings were starting to come back. Through ongoing counseling—including one week-long intensive on anger, shame, and unforgivenness, plus another week in another place—through reading some pivotal books, receiving love from some wonderful friends . . . life was returning.

I'll come back to that, but before I do, I want to share with you something that happened before I moved.

One afternoon I went to the theater, alone, trying to distract me from myself for a while. I skimmed the posters in the lobby, stopping at *Never Let Me Go*. The copy boasted a quote from *TIME*: "Adapted from the best novel of the decade." That was good enough for me. I bought my ticket and my popcorn and settled into my seat.

This 2010 film was an adaptation of Kazuo Ishiguro's sci-fi story of a group of English boarding school students who learn they are clones created specifically for organ harvesting. In confronting their own mortality, three classmates struggle to come to terms with their fate while grappling with love and what it means to be human.

I saw it three times—this first occasion, when the place was almost empty, it brought tears to my eyes. I loved everything about it—the cinematography, the writing, the directing, the acting, the soundtrack.

My daughter had been living in the same city, and she had just told me her husband had gotten a job that would be moving them to North Carolina. I invited them to the movie as a way of saying good-bye. The final scene shows Kathy, played by Carey Mulligan, getting out of her car and standing by a barbed-wire fence that's caught some roadside litter. Looking out across an open field, she says in a voiceover:

I come here and imagine that this is the spot where everything I've lost since my childhood is washed out. I tell myself, if that were true, and I waited long enough, then a tiny figure would appear on the horizon across the field and gradually get larger until I'd see it was Tommy. He'd wave. And maybe call. I don't know if the fantasy will go beyond that, I can't let it. I remind myself I was lucky to have had any time with him at all. What I'm not sure about, is, if our lives have been so different from the lives of the people we save. We all complete ["die"]. Maybe none of us really understand what we've lived through, or feel we've had enough time.

The last two sentences devastated me. Outside I gave my daughter a poster of the movie. With tears flowing down my cheeks I hugged them both, told them I loved them, and told them good-bye.

Many people didn't like the film, didn't understand it, and couldn't recommend it. Many critics didn't either. I did understand it, at least on a subconscious level, but I couldn't explain it. It was as if my heart understood but my mind didn't. So I did some research, reading reviews, both of the film and of the book. When I came across a review by M. John Harrison in *The Guardian*, my mind finally understood what my heart couldn't express:

It's about the steady erosion of hope. It's about repressing what you know, which is that in this life people fail one another, grow old and fall to pieces. It's about knowing that while you must keep calm, keeping calm won't change a thing. Beneath Kathy's flattened and lukewarm emotional landscape lies the pure volcanic turmoil, the unexpressed yet perfectly articulated, perfectly molten rage of the orphan. . . .

This extraordinary and, in the end, rather frighteningly clever novel isn't about cloning, or being a clone, at all. It's about why we don't explode, why we don't just wake up one day and go sobbing and crying down the street, kicking everything to pieces out of the raw, infuriating, completely personal sense of our lives never having been what they could have been.

The reviewer felt what I had felt only he had the words to describe it.

I knew I didn't have forever with my daughter and son-in-law, but I didn't think they would be gone so soon. I didn't think any of my kids would be gone so soon. Perhaps that's why I sobbed on the curb under the streetlight of my old neighborhood. It was all over so quickly. My childhood. My children's childhood. Where did they go? How did both slip away so fast?

I agree with the critic who reviewed the book. I truly don't know why all of us "don't just wake up one day and go sobbing and crying down the street, kicking everything to pieces out of the raw, infuriating, completely personal sense of our lives never having been what they could have been." What puzzles me is I don't have friends who feel that way, or, if they do, I haven't heard them express those feelings. Which makes me feel even more of an outsider. Is it just highly sensitive people who feel this way? Is it only artists and writers and filmmakers? Is something wrong with me, or is something wrong with the rest of the world? Am I out of touch with reality, or are they?

I felt I had wasted so much of my life. "We all *complete*," as Carey Mulligan's character says, a euphemism for dying. "Maybe none of us really understand what we've lived through, or feel we've had enough time."

Truly, I *was* just beginning to understand the life I'd lived. And, tragically, there wasn't enough time to sort through all the memories, to re-mat them with perspective, reframe them with forgiveness, hang them in a place where they catch the light just right so they can be seen the way they were meant to be seen.

□ □ □ ▓

So, back to my story: I was staying in Oklahoma City this past year with one of my daughters as she was starting a business. One day I decided to drive to Fort Worth to see my sister and her two children, who are hardly children anymore. Both are married; one has a child of her own.

I took I-35, going south, which meant I would be entering Fort Worth from the north. I hadn't thought about this until I actually crossed the city limits, but the north side of town was where my dad had coached football. I started seeing familiar street signs, like "NW 28th," and I remembered we took that street to get to Zion Lutheran Church. The drive seemed forever as a kid. I remembered the petroleum storage tanks and the runoff fumes spewing from the top. I hadn't thought of that smell since I was a kid.

I reflected on the fun times I had with my dad. He introduced me to the world he worked in, and I remember feeling a sense of privilege about this. He took me into locker rooms, introduced me, had me shake hands with co-workers— you know, man things. I always felt safe in that world because Dad ruled it.

He took me to the Golden Gloves fights in the Will Rogers Auditorium. After football season some players fought there. It was a shadowy place that felt as if you'd fallen into some black-and-white scene from another era. Hot lights beamed down on the canvas square in the center, cordoned off by ropes. The place reeked of cigarettes and cigars and things cooked in hot oil. Mostly men were there, sitting in folding chairs, standing during moments of high drama. Applauding. Booing sometimes. I think that was the first time I heard booing at a sporting event.

It was startling how everything came so vibrantly back to life.

As I drove, my mind traveled around the city of my youth, my adolescence, and my early adulthood. Thoughts glanced off the tops of the memories, none staying too long before darting off to another. TCU on the southwest side. I loved college. Well . . . I loved my college *friends*. Loved playing handball and basketball, doing Young Life work. Loved not having the pressure to date, because I didn't have the time or the money, which was probably a good thing.

I loved seeing God show up in the lives of high school kids. My freshman year, I worked with a really smart friend who knew a lot about the Bible. I didn't. And I remembered that with a smile now, how I used to pray silently at some of the club meetings, *God, please, if anyone has any questions, have them ask Jackie.*

East Belknap, the first apartment my wife and I had after we got married. The Jane Lane Apartments. Two bedrooms at first, one for us, one for my study; then three the next year when our daughter came. There was that place we ate ribs sometimes, what was it called? Sammy's? Or was it Coors BBQ?

Before I knew it, I had circled the city in my mind.

I arrived at my sister's just in time to leave for dinner in Dallas with her kids and their spouses. I had brought a gift for the one-year-old daughter and was excited to see them all. As I watched them talk and interact I recalled moments with them both when they were little. I was talking with my niece about my daughter and tears welled in my eyes when I thought of what a good mom she was.

When I got back in the car with my sister, the dammed-up emotions burst. "What's wrong?" she asked.

"I can't believe they grew up so fast. I missed so much of their lives. I've wasted so many opportunities with them."

"They adore you, Ken," she said consolingly.

After my emotions ran their course, we had a great talk. When we arrived back at her place, I got ready for bed, and, heading for the bathroom, almost stepped on something. I picked it up. It was a small leaf. Reddish. Fully formed and whole. And it was in the shape of a heart.

"Look at this," I said, showing her.

She marveled at it too. "It's a sign," she said, smiling. "Of new beginnings."

"That would be nice."

"Do you know what today is?"

"No."

"December 3rd. Dad's birthday."

It was a palpable, almost transcendent moment.

The next day I went to see a friend I'd known since college. I called ahead to ask if he would meet to help me understand what God was doing in my life. He understands me, loves me, and is one of the wisest people I know. I sat at his office conference table, and he wrote on a whiteboard. He asked if I knew what a meta-narrative was. I did. It's the larger story that overarches all the smaller stories in our life, giving them context and meaning.

"What is the meta-narrative of your life?" he asked.

"Well, I wake up every morning with one thing I pray before I get out of bed, and that is my meta-narrative. I first thank God for the gift of another day, then I ask: 'Please help me to love Jesus more at the end of the day than I do right now. And help me to love him more tomorrow than I do at the end of today. And help me love him more the day after tomorrow than tomorrow. And help me love him that way until at last I see him face-to-face and fall into his arms.'"

Knowing me, he concurred, and jotted down a summary of my words. We talked a lot, while he marked the board and I wrote in my notebook.

He asked about my hopes for the future and had me examine how those hopes were being realized. Then he asked: "What do you fear?"

"I don't fear a lot of things," I said. "But the one thing I do fear is wasting my life."

He wrote that on the board. Then he drew a diagram of an hourglass. At the top half he wrote: "Hopes for the future." At the bottom: "Hopes fulfilled." Then, next to the constricting middle: "Wasted life."

He explained. "In order for the hopes you have up here to get down there, they have to pass here," he said, pointing to the "Wasted life" constriction.

He stepped back and paused. I wasn't sure where he was going with it, but then he said: "What constitutes a wasted life?"

"Well, I think it's something that isn't meaningful, doesn't last, doesn't help anyone."

"Do you think you've wasted your life?"

"I just feel I've made so many mistakes, failed so many people, including God."

"The difference between guilt and shame is this: Guilt says 'I screwed up.' Shame says 'I'm a screw-up.' You made some mistakes, Ken, but *you* are not a mistake. You have loved and helped so many people. You haven't wasted your life. But the shame you have over your failures makes it feel that way."

I nodded, taking it all in, understanding the truth of what he was saying.

"How can any of us tell if we have wasted our life? We can't judge the smaller failures in our story unless we know the whole of the larger story and how those failures fit into the big picture."

I thought of Lazarus outside the rich man's gate. Who had the wasted life? It depends what the overarching narrative is. In the world's eyes it was Lazarus who wasted his life. In God's eyes, it was the rich man.

I thought of the thief on the cross. He likely would have said he had wasted his life, and yet, if you look at how his smaller story played out in the larger story of redemption, there's no telling how many people are with Jesus in paradise because in a deathbed plea they called out to him as the thief had.

Who of us can see the whole of our story in a way that qualifies us to judge the smaller scenes within it? Who knows the impact of a cup of water given in Jesus' name? Who knows how a prayer prayed in private plays itself out over generations? A gift given in secret? An act of devotion?

Albert Schweitzer wrote: "It is not always granted to the sower to see the harvest. All worthwhile work is done in faith."

We *sow* seeds. We can't make seeds. We can't guarantee seeds. We can't control seeds, in terms of which will germinate and when, or which will produce fruit and how much. We plant;

God causes the growth. We sow in faith and trust God with whatever comes up.

We love, we laugh, we give, we receive, we hope, we pray. We fail, others fail us. We shame others, others shame us. We hurt others, others hurt us. We get angry, we withhold love, friendship, and forgiveness. We fall, we get up. We help others get up. We weep. We wonder about the meaning of it all, the use of it, the waste of it. Along the way we find bits of bread that guide us and feed us, a little at a time. And, somehow, with the help of our friends, we find our way home.

I can't explain how I felt when I left my friend's office, other than that I carried a tremendous energy, as if blood flow had finally been reestablished to a part of my heart that for much of its life had been deprived. I felt, to use Brené Brown's terminology, "wholehearted."

One quote she uses in her book is from theologian Howard Thurman: "Don't ask what the world needs. Ask what makes you come alive, and go do it. Because what the world needs is people who have come alive."

I had, for all of my life, lived the opposite.

□ □ □ ▪

When I stopped to say good-bye to my sister, she had framed the heart-shaped leaf.

It wasn't dark yet, and I decided, on a lark, to take one last drive down the streets of my youth, the schools I had attended, the way I walked home from school, the old neighborhood, and the neighborhood we moved to after we left that one. I cried but didn't feel sadness or regret or pain of any kind. Only gratitude.

In T. S. Eliot's series of poems titled *Four Quartets*, this is
my favorite part:

At the end of all our exploring
Will be to arrive where we started
And know the place for the first time.

Perhaps it is true what Thomas Wolfe once said, that we can't
go home again.

But perhaps in a way it is also true that none of us can keep
from going back.

I went back to my old neighborhood a lot over the years,
mostly by myself, and mostly just taking it all in. I'm not sure
why I kept coming. For understanding, perhaps. Or forgiveness—of what there was to give of it and what there was to
receive. Part of why I kept returning, I think, was to finally be
able to unclench my hands and let something go. In so doing
I was able to open my hands and let something come—a gift.

That gift was my wholeness.

Here is what I have learned.

I have learned that God allows painful memories from our
past to come back to us, to each and every one of us, because
he cares about the little boy back there, whose soul is sitting on
a curb with a freshly skinned knee, desperately trying to hide
from the other boys how much it hurts. He has compassion for
the little girl whose heart is buried in a pillow that silently blots
her unspoken pain. God so loves the hurt little child within us
that he doesn't want the hurts to keep hurting us. In his own
time and in his own way, he comes to those hurts. One by one
he touches them. And with his touch comes healing.

I have learned that what the world needs is wholehearted people, people who have come alive. And, once alive, we are to go among the bruised reeds and dimly burning wicks to share this life.

I have learned that we were meant to live outside the gate of the city and inside the door of God's heart. Outside is where the truth of the human condition is. Inside is where the joy of the divine heart is. The truth on the outside enables us to experience the joy on the inside without hoarding it. The joy on the inside gives us the strength to bear the truth on the outside without hiding from it.

□ □ □　■

You can never say you have wasted your life, nor can I.

All worthwhile work is done in faith, and none of us knows enough of the larger story to judge our own story, let alone the stories of others.

Ask what makes you come alive.

And go pursue it.

Relentlessly.

FOR DISCUSSION AND STUDY

1. A character in *Never Let Me Go* says, "We all complete [die]. Maybe none of us really understand what we've lived through, or feel we've had enough time." Have you ever been reflective and emotional to where you've wondered if your life has meant anything at all to anyone? If it has been anywhere close to what it could have been? If you have had these kinds of thoughts, what were you experiencing at the time that might have precipitated them? What is it that you feel you haven't had enough time for?

2. What do you see as being the difference between guilt and shame? How have guilt and/or shame impacted and shaped your life up to the present time?

3. What have you worked on and persevered through entirely by faith, seeing neither effects nor results?

4. What would it mean for you to more fully enter into your own story, or to paraphrase Brené Brown, to walk into your experiences and start living and loving with your whole heart? *What makes you come alive?*

5. What decisions could you make and actions could you take to start down this path? *How will you pursue relentlessly?*

EPILOGUE

Coming Home

With some this pursuit of God is swift and decisive; and so a
Magdalene becomes at once a woman of saintliest ways, a Saul
stands forth as the world-grasping Paul, to whom "to live is
Christ, and to die is gain" . . . a Spanish cavalier is hurled by a
cannonball into the saintliness of Ignatius.

With others God's task is harder, the pursuit is longer.

—Francis Peter Le Buffe
The Hound of Heaven: An Interpretation

Each year the Coast Guard saves around five thousand people
(sometimes more) from drowning. During the devastating
2005 hurricane season, they rescued or evacuated more than
thirty-three thousand whose lives had been threatened by Katrina.

In 1984, a cargo ship lost thirty-one crew members in a raging
storm on the Eastern Seaboard; at the time, the Navy had only
one helicopter unit to assist in the rescue attempt. Congress
then established a new Coast Guard program called the Rescue

Swimmers. The men and women of its elite and highly successful yet little-known team, on a moment's notice, are called upon to drop from helicopters and plunge into storm-tossed seas to rescue those in danger. Their training is considered the toughest in all the military; nearly half who enter drop out.

The film *The Guardian* gives an inside look at the heart and soul of these rarely glimpsed professionals dedicated to the motto "So Others May Live!" The storyline goes something like this: After losing his crew in a crash, the renowned swimmer Ben Randall (Kevin Costner) is forced to step down from rescue work to teach Coast Guard Rescue Swimmers. There he encounters blue-chip swimmer Jake Fischer (Ashton Kutcher), who is determined to break all his instructor's records.

One by one, he does.

But Ben is a legend among his peers, and stories of his quiet heroism haunt Jake. The self-confident upstart discovers that Ben keeps a number in his head, a number he assumes to represent the people Ben has saved during his career. Several times he tries to pry it from the man, but it isn't something Ben wants to discuss.

Meanwhile, Jake is equally enigmatic to Ben: Why would this Olympic-caliber athlete choose the Coast Guard over a college scholarship? The kid is likewise an outsider, and Ben knows that to bring him inside, he must learn what put him where he is. With a little digging, he discovers Jake carries a secret, the source of his shame. He had been behind the wheel of a car in which several on his swim team were killed.

Ben calls him into his office one evening and says, "I've read the report, Jake. Your blood alcohol level was zip that night. I'm guessing there was a flip for designated driver; you lost."

"I guess that just makes it all go away, huh?"

"No, it doesn't make it all right; it just makes it an accident. At least that's how it reads. You were sixteen years old, Jake. I'm not your priest, but if I was, I think maybe you deserve a pass."

Jake is angry now, his voice steadily rising. "You're giving me a pass. You think you know everything, with your psychobabble bulls—. Why am I here? Why are you here, huh? You're too old to be doing this; you washed up here. You don't want to be teaching a bunch of kids in a pool, am I right? I don't give a f—what you read or who you talked to! You don't know about me!" He pauses to collect himself: "I have *me* under control."

"I can see that. The only difference between you and me is that I don't wear the ones I lost on my arm. I know where you're at, Jake. I'm there myself. I ask myself every day why I was the one who survived."

"And?"

"And if I can't answer that for me, I'm certainly not going to try to answer that for you. Have a seat. I want you to start being a member of this team. The team you have now. You have a gift, Jake. You're the best swimmer to come through this program, hands down, by far, and you've got a whole record board to prove it. But you know what I see when I look at it? I see someone fast enough who's going to get there first. I see someone strong enough who's going to last. I see someone who can save a life maybe no one else could. You really want to honor the initials on your arm? Then honor your gift. Save the ones you can, Jake. The rest, you've got to let go."

That moment of understanding and compassion proves to be a turning point. Jake becomes less focused on himself, more on his teammates. Shortly after he graduates, he visits Ben and they talk over beers.

"Hey, there was a question I wanted to ask you back at school, but I didn't. When you can't save 'em all, how do you choose who lives?"

"It's probably different for everybody, Jake. It's kind of simple for me, though. I just take the first one I come to, or the weakest one in the group, and then I swim as fast and as hard as I can for as long as I can. And the sea takes the rest."

Jake then presses. "What's your real number?"

"Twenty-two."

Much lower than Jake imagined. "Twenty-two? That's not bad. It's not two hundred, but—"

"Twenty-two is the number of people I *lost,* Jake. The only number I kept track of."

□ □□ ■

The sign over Jesus' cross could well have read "So Others May Live!"

In relentlessly pursuing each and every one of us, Jesus swam as fast as he could, as hard as he could, for as long as he could. Reaching for the nearest, the weakest.

But though he desires all to be saved, all are not saved.

Only one of the drowning men next to Jesus reached out to him.

The sea took the other one.

If there is a number Jesus keeps track of, my guess is it's not of the ones saved but the ones lost. He takes any such loss hard. Why else would he have wept so bitterly when approaching Jerusalem for the last time before he died?

Probably you are among the ninety-nine who are saved, and not the one who is lost. Even so, perhaps a part of you is lost. It may be a small part, even a seemingly insignificant part. Maybe it's just 1 percent.

Look at that number. Look at the one part of you that is far from Jesus—whether it's shame or anger or unforgivenness, judgmentalism, self-righteousness, or whatever.

That one part is far *from him.*

Think about this.

Do you really want that? Do you want any part of you to be far from the One who loves you the way only he does, the One who is able and willing to forgive you of anything, time and again, over and over and over again? Do you want *any* part of you to be far from the One who sacrificed everything for you—for all of you, for every last part of you? Do you want any part of you to be far from the One who is willing to give you any good thing, to the point that his generosity is infinitely beyond what you can imagine?

As he has done for me, the Good Shepherd has come a very long way for the one part of you that is lost—the one part that's alone, and in danger.

Call to him. Call to him out of your loneliness. Call to him out of your brokenness. Call to him through your tears and your trembling lips. But call to him. Let him know you need him, and let him know how much. Let him know you miss him. And that you want to come home.

He *will* find you. That is who he is. That is what he does. Again, even if it's just one part of you that is lost, *you* are worth it.

You are so relentlessly worth it.

And when that shivering part of you is found, he will put you on his shoulders and carry you. That you are safe, that you are close, that you are on your way to wholeness, will fill him with great joy.

Along the way, he will talk to you, tenderly.

And at the end of the way, he will take you inside, where you will be welcomed to take part in his joy.

In his most beautiful name, I pray it might be so . . . for both of us. Amen.

APPENDIX

The Hound of Heaven

Francis, your poem is magnificent. That is the only word I can think of. It is a difficult poem, and I will need to read it several more times. But even though I don't understand every verse, I'm powerfully affected, and I truly want to read it again—it's a masterpiece. An opulent jewel of a poem.

—Robert Waldron
The Hound of Heaven at My Heels:
The Lost Diaries of Francis Thompson

Thompson's poem is difficult to read in places, not to mention difficult to understand. Its figures of speech are from a more literary era, and many of its subtleties are lost on a contemporary audience. Everyone then knew the Bible, for example, even those who didn't believe it, and allusions to scriptural images were widely and readily understood. Also, poetry was more formal, with careful attention to rhyme and meter. Since Walt Whitman, poetry has broken ranks from the more regimented lines of iambic pentameter to follow the more sauntering cadences of blank verse and free verse.

If poetry has been difficult for you, you're not alone. It can be less so if you gain an understanding of the form and how it has been traditionally used. A poem is an economical way of telling a story, often just a fragment of a story. Thompson's poem is a good example. Usually a poem captures a moment and the thought or feeling that moment aroused in the poet. In this sense, it will not do what a short story does, let alone a novel. Poetry is a small, carefully crafted art form—like a brooch, a filigree of finely wrought words inlaid with a precisely cut jewel, the facets of which reflect some personal or universal truth.

Of course, not everyone likes brooches. Some are overwrought to the point of being gaudy. Even at its gaudiest, though, poetry is essential to society, for it speaks of sacred things with deference, even reverence. And where can you go in today's world to hear such things so spoken?

I have always loved the music of Simon & Garfunkel, because they speak of those things with such soft-spoken voices. "All Things Wait to Be Noticed" is an Art Garfunkel song, and that is what poets do best, I think. They help us notice things, especially quiet and shy things that whisper to us about all that is good and true and beautiful in the world, in other people, in us. Poets teach us to pay attention. By the way they look they show *us* how to look. By the way they listen, they show *us* how to listen, how to think, how to feel, how to walk in a world lush with soft-petaled things, things that can be easily crushed underfoot if we're not careful.

□ □ □　■

Robert Waldron wrote a fictionalized account of Francis Thompson's life in *The Hound of Heaven at My Heels: The Lost Diary of Francis Thompson*. He concludes his novel with these words, which I think capture the heart of God for the outsider:

> Many teachers of Thompson have failed to inform us that he was an addict most of his life. Perhaps they fear this unpleasant truth can distract some from appreciating the man's genius or tempt others to sin. Surely they want their students to emulate his spiritual strength and not his physical weakness. But knowing that he struggled with opium addiction all his life renders him in my eyes more heroic—and more human. Thompson's life says to all of us: No matter how many times we fail, God will never fail us. He knows our frailty and loves us still, pursuing us relentlessly as a lover his beloved.

For a more present-day rendering of the poem, you might listen to the song "Hound of Heaven" by Michael Card, who translates Thompson's poem into lyrics that capture its heart in a clear, concise, and compelling way.

For an analysis of the poem, I have two recommendations: A shorter treatment is *I Fled Him, Down the Nights and Down the Days: The Text of The Hound of Heaven* by Francis Thompson with photographic commentary by Algimantas Kezys, and the text with interpretive commentary by John F. Quinn (Chicago: Loyola University Press, 1970).

In this work, Quinn writes: " 'The Hound of Heaven' is one of the great, if not the greatest lyrical poems in the English language. For sublimity of thought, power of expression, beauty of imagery, and verse melody, all of which qualities are to be sought in a great poem, it is unsurpassed by any of the masterpieces of our greatest English lyricists."

A longer treatment is *The Hound of Heaven: An Interpretation* by Francis Peter Le Buffe.

I love this quote from the latter source:

We have all "fled Him, down the nights and days" and the poem smites on our souls as did the handwriting on Balthasar's walls. As you read and ponder, there resound within our hearts the accusing words of the Prophet Nathan to King David: "Thou art the man." . . . Against its poignant throbbings we lay our own hearts "to beat and share the commingling heat"; and it is quite safe to say that many a prayer has been breathed and many a heart moved to take at least initial steps to end its flight from God, as line after line awakened memories that burned and seared the soul unto its own healing.

Earlier I quoted the first and last parts of *The Hound of Heaven*; here it is in its entirety. Most readers find it rough sledding in places, and, if you find it such, may I suggest enriching your experience through an online search for: Richard Burton, "The Hound of Heaven." There you should find a recorded reading by this classically trained stage actor that lends a sense of the poem's rhyme and meter and helps with pronunciation of antiquated terms. As Burton recites, follow along silently, reading the lines below:

> *I FLED Him, down the nights and down the days;*
> *I fled Him, down the arches of the years;*
> *I fled Him, down the labyrinthine ways*
> *Of my own mind; and in the mist of tears*
> *I hid from Him, and under running laughter.*
> *Up vistaed hopes I sped;*
> *And shot, precipitated,*

Adown Titanic glooms of chasmèd fears,
    From those strong Feet that followed, followed after.
        But with unhurrying chase,
        And unperturbèd pace,
    Deliberate speed, majestic instancy,
        They beat—and a Voice beat
        More instant than the Feet—
"All things betray thee, who betrayest Me."

        I pleaded, outlaw-wise,
By many a hearted casement, curtained red,
    Trellised with intertwining charities;
(For, though I knew His love Who followèd,
        Yet was I sore adread
Lest, having Him, I must have naught beside).
But, if one little casement parted wide,
    The gust of His approach would clash it to.
Fear wist not to evade, as Love wist to pursue.
Across the margent of the world I fled,
    And troubled the gold gateways of the stars,
    Smiting for shelter on their clangèd bars;
        Fretted to dulcet jars
And silvern chatter the pale ports o' the moon.
I said to Dawn: Be sudden—to Eve: Be soon;
    With thy young skiey blossoms heap me over
        From this tremendous Lover—
Float thy vague veil about me, lest He see!
I tempted all His servitors, but to find
My own betrayal in their constancy,
    In faith to Him their fickleness to me,
        Their traitorous trueness, and their loyal deceit.
To all swift things for swiftness did I sue;
    Clung to the whistling mane of every wind.
        But whether they swept, smoothly fleet,

The long savannahs of the blue;
  Or whether, Thunder-driven,
  They clanged his chariot 'thwart a heaven,
Flashy with flying lightnings round the spurn o' their
  feet:—
Fear wist not to evade as Love wist to pursue.
    Still with unhurrying chase,
    And unperturbèd pace,
  Deliberate speed, majestic instancy,
    Came on the following Feet,
    And a Voice above their beat—
  "Naught shelters thee, who wilt not shelter Me."

I sought no more that after which I strayed
    In face of man or maid;
But still within the little children's eyes
    Seems something, something that replies,
They at least are for me, surely for me!
I turned me to them very wistfully;
But just as their young eyes grew sudden fair
    With dawning answers there,
Their angel plucked them from me by the hair.
"Come then, ye other children, Nature's—share
With me" (said I) "your delicate fellowship;
    Let me greet you lip to lip,
    Let me twine with you caresses,
      Wantoning
    With our Lady-Mother's vagrant tresses,
      Banqueting
    With her in her wind-walled palace,
    Underneath her azured daïs,
    Quaffing, as your taintless way is,
      From a chalice

Lucent-weeping out of the dayspring."
    So it was done:
I in their delicate fellowship was one—
Drew the bolt of Nature's secrecies.
    I knew all the swift importings
    On the wilful face of skies;
    I knew how the clouds arise
    Spumèd of the wild sea-snortings;
        All that's born or dies
    Rose and drooped with; made them shapers
Of mine own moods, or wailful or divine;
    With them joyed and was bereaven.
    I was heavy with the even,
    When she lit her glimmering tapers
    Round the day's dead sanctities.
    I laughed in the morning's eyes.
I triumphed and I saddened with all weather,
    Heaven and I wept together,
And its sweet tears were salt with mortal mine;
Against the red throb of its sunset-heart
        I laid my own to beat,
        And share commingling heat;
But not by that, by that, was eased my human smart.
In vain my tears were wet on Heaven's grey cheek.
For ah! we know not what each other says,
    These things and I; in sound I speak—
Their sound is but their stir, they speak by silences.
Nature, poor stepdame, cannot slake my drouth;
    Let her, if she would owe me,
Drop yon blue bosom-veil of sky, and show me
    The breasts o' her tenderness:
Never did any milk of hers once bless
        My thirsting mouth.

Nigh and nigh draws the chase,
With unperturbèd pace,
Deliberate speed, majestic instancy;
And past those noisèd Feet
A voice comes yet more fleet—
"Lo! naught contents thee, who content'st not Me!"
Naked I wait Thy love's uplifted stroke!
My harness piece by piece Thou hast hewn from me,
And smitten me to my knee;
I am defenceless utterly.
I slept, methinks, and woke,
And, slowly gazing, find me stripped in sleep.
In the rash lustihead of my young powers,
I shook the pillaring hours
And pulled my life upon me; grimed with smears,
I stand amid the dust o' the mounded years—
My mangled youth lies dead beneath the heap.
My days have crackled and gone up in smoke,
Have puffed and burst as sun-starts on a stream.
Yea, faileth now even dream
The dreamer, and the lute the lutanist;
Even the linked fantasies, in whose blossomy twist
I swung the earth a trinket at my wrist,
Are yielding; cords of all too weak account
For earth with heavy griefs so overplussed.
Ah! is Thy love indeed
A weed, albeit an amaranthine weed,
Suffering no flowers except its own to mount?
Ah! must—
Designer infinite!—
Ah! must Thou char the wood ere Thou canst limn with it?
My freshness spent its wavering shower i' the dust;
And now my heart is as a broken fount,

Wherein tear-drippings stagnate, spilt down ever
From the dank thoughts that shiver
Upon the sighful branches of my mind.
Such is; what is to be?
The pulp so bitter, how shall taste the rind?
I dimly guess what Time in mists confounds;
Yet ever and anon a trumpet sounds
From the hid battlements of Eternity;
Those shaken mists a space unsettle, then
Round the half-glimpsèd turrets slowly wash again.
But not ere him who summoneth
I first have seen, enwound
With glooming robes purpureal, cypress-crowned;
His name I know, and what his trumpet saith.
Whether man's heart or life it be which yields
Thee harvest, must Thy harvest-fields
Be dunged with rotten death?

Now of that long pursuit
Comes on at hand the bruit;
That Voice is round me like a bursting sea:
"And is thy earth so marred,
Shattered in shard on shard?
Lo, all things fly thee, for thou fliest Me!
Strange, piteous, futile thing!
Wherefore should any set thee love apart?
Seeing none but I makes much of naught" (He said),
"And human love needs human meriting:
How hast thou merited—
Of all man's clotted clay the dingiest clot?
Alack, thou knowest not
How little worthy of any love thou art!
Whom wilt thou find to love ignoble thee,
Save Me, save only Me?

All which I took from thee I did but take,
  Not for thy harms,
But just that thou might'st seek it in My arms.
  All which thy child's mistake
Fancies as lost, I have stored for thee at home:
  Rise, clasp My hand, and come!"
  Halts by me that footfall:
  Is my gloom, after all,
Shade of His hand, outstretched caressingly?
  "Ah, fondest, blindest, weakest,
  I am He Whom thou seekest!
Thou dravest love from thee, who dravest Me."

NOTES

Epigraph

page 6   Robert Waldron, *The Hound of Heaven at My Heels: The Lost Diaries of Francis Thompson* (San Francisco: Ignatius, 1999), 90.

Prologue: Leaving Home

page 9   Francis Peter Le Buffe, *The Hound of Heaven: An Interpretation* (New York: Macmillan, 1921), 6.

page 13   S. E. Hinton, *The Outsiders* (New York: Viking Juvenile, 40th Anniversary Edition, 2007), 176.

Chapter 1: The Pursuit

page 19   Le Buffe, *The Hound of Heaven: An Interpretation*, 25.

page 23   For more on Eugene O'Neill and Dorothy Day, see William D. Miller, *Dorothy Day: A Biography* (San Francisco: Harper & Row, 1982), 103–118; Jim Forest, *Love Is the Measure: A Biography of Dorothy Day* (New York: Paulist, 1986), 41–42; Dorothy Day, *The Long Loneliness* (New York: Harper & Row, 1981); Patrick Jordan, ed., *Dorothy Day: Writings from Commonweal* (Collegeville, MN: The Liturgical Press, 2002), 44–45.

page 27   John Kelman, *Among Famous Books* (Ithaca: Cornell University Library, 2009), 311.

Chapter 2: The Pursuer

page 29   The epigraph is from an interview of Anne Lamott with Ed Underwood. Accessed: at www.jesusmovementblog.com/2010/07/21/best-conversion-story-anne-lamott.

page 29   The story of Anne Lamott's conversion is from Anne Lamott, *Traveling Mercies* (New York: Anchor, 2000), 44–50.

page 35   Margaret Wise Brown, *The Runaway Bunny*, illustrated by Clement Hurd (New York: HarperCollins, rev. ed., 2005).
page 37   Frederick Buechner, *The Hungering Dark* (San Francisco: HarperSanFrancisco, 1967), 14.

Chapter 3: The Nature of the Pursuit

page 41   C. S. Lewis, *Surprised by Joy* (New York: Houghton Mifflin Harcourt, rev. ed., 1995), 221.
page 44   *They Stand Together: The Letters of C. S. Lewis to Arthur Greeves* (1914–1963), Walter Hooper, ed. (New York: Macmillan, 1979), letter dated October 12, 1916.
page 45   Lewis, *Surprised by Joy*.
page 46   Lewis, *Surprised by Joy*, 185.
page 47   C. S. Lewis, *Mere Christianity* (San Francisco: HarperSanFrancisco, 2001), 199.
page 48   Ibid.

Chapter 4: The Part of Us That Is Lost

page 61   Brené Brown DVD, *The Hustle for Worthiness: Exploring the Power of Love, Belonging and Being Enough*.
page 62   Ibid.
page 62   Brené Brown, *The Gifts of Imperfection* (Center City, MN: Hazelden, 2010), 68.
page 64   Bion of Borysthenes, quoted in John Bartlett and Justin Kaplan, *Bartlett's Familiar Quotations* (New York: Little, Brown and Co., 17th ed., 2002), 81.
page 70   *The Dictionary of Biblical Imagery* (Downers Grove, IL: InterVarsity, 1998).

Chapter 5: God's Passion for the Outsider

page 81   Howard Macy, *Rhythms of the Inner Life* (Colorado Springs: Chariot Victor, 1999), chap. 1.
page 82   Frank Anthony Spina, *The Faith of the Outsider* (Grand Rapids: Eerdmans, 2005), 9–10.
page 83   Edwin Markham, "Outwitted," cited in *The Best Loved Poems of the American People* (New York: Doubleday, 2008), 66.
page 85   Gregory A. Boyd, *Repenting of Religion: Turning from Judgment to the Love of God* (Grand Rapids: Baker Books, 2004), 174.
page 86   Ibid.

Chapter 6: God's Provision for the Outsider

page 97   Henri J.M. Nouwen, *Reaching Out: The Three Movements of the Spiritual Life* (New York: Doubleday, 1975), 71.
page 99   Ibid., 52.

page 100 Nouwen, *Reaching Out*, 81.
page 100 Ibid., 73.
page 102 Richard Kearney, *Anatheism* (New York: Columbia University Press, 2011), 19.
page 103 Ibid., 21.

Chapter 7: Jesus' Mission to the Outsider

page 108 Spina, *The Faith of the Outsider*, 51.
page 109 Ibid., 71.
page 110 Spina, *The Faith of the Outsider*, 6.
page 112 Ibid., 139.

Chapter 8: God's Mandate to the Insider

page 135 Steve Lopez, *The Soloist* (New York: The Penguin Group, 2008).
page 136 From *The Soloist*, a Paramount picture, 2009, directed by Joe Wright, written by Steve Lopez and Suzannah Grant, starring Jamie Foxx and Robert Downey Jr.

Chapter 9: The Part of Me That Was Found

page 139 From the Brené Brown DVD, *The Hustle for Worthiness*.
page 141 From *Never Let Me Go*, a 20th Century Fox picture, 2010, directed by Mark Romanek, written by Alex Garland and Kazuo Ishiguro, starring Keira Knightley, Carey Mulligan, and Andrew Garfield.
page 149 T. S. Eliot, "The Four Quartets," from *Collected Poems* (New York: Harcourt, Brace, Jovanovich, 1991), 59.

Epilogue: Coming Home

page 153 Francis Peter Le Buffe, *The Hound of Heaven: An Interpretation*, 9.
page 154 Paraphrased storyline of *The Guardian*, DVD, Buena Vista Home Entertainment/Touchstone, 2007, starring Kevin Costner, Ashton Kutcher, and Sela Ward.

Appendix: *The Hound of Heaven*

page 159 Waldron, *The Hound of Heaven at My Heels: The Lost Diaries of Francis Thompson*, 75.
page 161 Ibid., 90.
page 161 John F. Quinn, quoted in *I Fled Him, Down the Nights and Down the Days: The Text of The Hound of Heaven* by Francis Thompson; photographic commentary by Algimantas Kezys; interpretive commentary and annotations by John F. Quinn (Chicago: Loyola University Press, 1970), n.p.
page 164 The poem, *The Hound of Heaven*, by Francis Thompson, is quoted in Le Buffe, *The Hound of Heaven: An Interpretation*, 19–25.

KEN GIRE (ThM, Dallas Theological Seminary) is the author of twenty-four books, four of which have sold over 100,000 copies each. He has won two ECPA Gold Medallion Awards. Ken teaches weekend seminars on writing throughout the country. He lives in Baltimore, Maryland. Visit his Facebook page under "Ken Gire, author."